Tangled World

ROGER
LINCOLN
SHINN

CHARLES SCRIBNER'S SONS   NEW YORK

Foreword

THIS BOOK DESCRIBES several areas of modern life in which our changing world demands decisions both of persons and of our entire society. I have picked out a few of the most striking problems and opportunities before us. Any reader can think of many that I have omitted.

The disturbing fact is that in each of these areas our society is constantly making decisions, often without knowing what it is doing. We are moving the world toward harmony or destruction, directing people toward prosperity or starvation, offering persons better working opportunities or consigning them to uselessness. Individuals and organizations make day-to-day decisions for the sake of immediate results, often with little thought that they are influencing momentous issues of our history. The purpose of the book is to help people understand what they are doing so that they can decide more responsibly.

I have no startling discoveries to announce. In many ways I am writing only about things that everybody knows—because everybody lives in this same world. But often we fail to notice what is going on. Or we are so thoroughly involved in what we are doing that we cannot see its relation to what other people are doing. Scientists and artists can often tell us things about ourselves and our world that we recognize as true, although we have missed seeing them. Some of their findings are reported here.

I have rarely prescribed answers to the questions I have raised—and for two reasons. First, there is not much usefulness in telling people what they ought to do. They are not likely to pay attention. But if they come to understand a situation and *discover* what they ought to do, they may then act on their insight. Second, often I do not know the answers. But as people in all walks of life become more aware of the problems before them, they can apply their skill to finding solutions.

This is not to say that knowledge alone will bring a better life. It won't. But as persons join knowledge to a sensitivity to human needs and to the basic loyalties of their lives, they can make responsible decisions. And responsible decisions are what our tangled world needs.

What follows is written out of certain Christian convictions, which are neither paraded nor hidden. Occasionally I emphasize them, because I believe it important for churchmen to realize that their faith demands intelligent participation in the many revolutions of our time. More often I do not elaborate these convictions, because I believe that men of diverse faiths frequently share ethical sensitivities that come to some through Christian faith.

This book is based on a series of television programs that appears under the same title. Most of the chapters incorporate parts of the scripts. But often I have put in my words what television reported through the camera or through my interviews with a variety of distinguished people. And in each chapter I have included more than could be squeezed into a half-hour television program.

R. L. S.

Contents

I | A World on the Move

IN THE TWENTIETH CENTURY a new kind of civilization has emerged in North America, parts of Europe, and scattered places around the world. Ideas, technology, visions, and loyalties have brought it into being. This new civilization is producing ways of life strikingly different from those of previous generations. Already it has transformed vast landscapes and patterns of behavior. And it is pregnant with possibilities for yet more far-reaching changes. It has made life both exhilarating and dangerous.

Although this emergent civilization is concentrated in one major part of the world, its effects reach out to all mankind. Africans who have never seen even a crude plow are accustomed to watching jet planes fly overhead. Around the world men seek freedom, economic advancement, a voice in determining the direction of history. All of us hear constant talk of revolutions—in politics, production of material goods, racial relations, population, communication, sexual behavior, urban living, and in almost anything else a person could mention. Clearly the world is on the move.

THE SHOCK OF CHANGE

Before examining some of the forms of this new style of civilization, we need to look at the bare fact of the impact of change itself. Although people often prefer to stay "set in their ways," they also may welcome change. But some kinds of change are bewildering and disturbing. People do not know how to respond to them because they do not understand what is happen-

7

ing. James Reston, the Washington Bureau chief of the *New York Times,* has described the situation in these words:

> Change is the biggest story in the world today, and we are not covering it adequately; change in the size and movement of our people; change in the nature, location, and availability of jobs; violent change in the cities and on the land; change in the relations between village and town, town and city, city and state, state and nation, and, of course, change in the relations between the empires that are falling and the empires that are rising, the old states that are going down and the new ones that are coming up.[1]

As Reston explains, the understanding of change requires much more than the information we normally get in the press. It requires investigation of the processes beneath the obvious facts. It requires also "the perspective of history, without which no man can understand our time, and few even endure it."[2]

In many respects, of course, change is an old story in human history. This globe spins on its axis every twenty-four hours. It speeds through its elliptical orbit around the sun every year. Our whole solar system is rushing in the general direction of a distant star. And all these motions go on within a galaxy that is on the move in an expanding universe. Nobody can chart all these movements absolutely because there are no fixed points in space. Yet this elaborate variety of movements does not make us dizzy. The changes are all continuous or rhythmic. We get used to the patterns of day and night, the sequence of the seasons. We know roughly what to expect and we are not disturbed.

History knows a second kind of change—the cataclysm. A catastrophe of nature or of warfare may wipe out civilization in a given area, or transform radically the lives of many people. Society cannot take such events in its stride. Violent destruction is possible in our time—and on a scale beyond anything in the past. That is one reason why we are uneasy.

But a still different kind of change makes our age unlike the past. We are engaged in a course of rapid, successive change.

---

[1] James Reston, "The Biggest Story in the World," *The New Republic* (May 4, 1963), p. 15. Reston's statement was first made in an address at the fiftieth anniversary of Columbia University's Graduate School of Journalism.

[2] *Ibid.,* p. 16.

Each event in it modifies habits and institutions, so as to multiply further events. The automobile, for example, is not simply a single, isolated object. As such, anybody can get used to it rather easily. But the automobile stimulates an endless sequence of developments. It affects the organization of the family, the methods of industry and agriculture, the conduct of war, habits of young people on dates, the layouts of cities and the appearance of the countryside, the patterns of government, the preservation and destruction of life.

In such a situation there is no return to normalcy. No one quite knows what normalcy is. The momentum of change is swift and powerful; it cleanses and pollutes; it raises up new monuments to human endeavor and overturns old ones. The direction and extent of change are unpredictable. The future offers possibilities of wealth, education, and human achievement beyond the grandest visions of the past. But, as Winson Churchill has said, "The stone age may return on the gleaming wings of science." We do not know what will happen, but we go on living, trying to discern directions, making decisions.

A newspaper report tells of the recent transformation of Japan, as that nation has moved from its postwar defeat and disillusion to its present dynamism. With the stimulating growth and modernization has come a bewilderment expressed in the words of one Japanese citizen: "But where is our dream? We don't know what we want and who we are; you can see it makes us afraid."

Most Americans, who like to think they know the answers, do not talk that way. We are the pioneers of freedom, of technology, and of the other forces that are remaking the world. The forward thrust is as natural to us as the atmosphere. But our political oratory, our racial hostilities, our crime and mental disease betray us. We too are quivering under the shock of change. We must make decisions faster than we know how.

HOW PERSONS MAKE DECISIONS

Sometimes people make decisions because they have to. A situation requires a choice, and people respond. Sometimes they make decisions because they want to. Imagination sees a new possibility and somebody sets out to realize it. All living is a matter of decisions, some trivial and some important.

In some decisions a person decides *what* he wants. He may want a meal, revenge, peace of mind. He decides to move toward an objective, a goal, or an end. Other decisions concern *methods* for achieving what one wants. The end is settled but the means for reaching it must be chosen. Most major decisions concern both means and ends. This is especially true in the modern world, where new techniques make new achievements possible and expand the wants of men.

What men want is not entirely an individual matter. Every person's desires are influenced by the society in which he lives. A few generations ago an American Indian might value eagle feathers above coins; the English settlers preferred the coins. Each preference rested in a social order which gave the specific objects their value.

Every society develops a set of attitudes, purposes, and symbols that form what may be called its *ethos*. The contemporary ethos (or spirit) is different from the medieval; the American ethos is different from the Chinese. One fundamental aspect of the ethos of a society is its *ethic*. The ethic includes the society's sensitivity to good and bad, to right and wrong, to the needs of others and the needs of the self.

I am not arguing that a person's ethic is *entirely* the product of a society. An individual may resist the ethic of his society. He may resent the obligations society imposes, or he may see beyond the society's prejudices to something better. But no individual can disregard the ethic of the society, just as no one can talk sensibly without using a language that the society provides.

Many factors enter into the ethic of a society and thereby influence the way it and the people within it make their decisions. These factors may work for good or for bad, as judged by standards beyond the social consensus, but they help to settle what the society thinks is good and bad. Among these factors are habits and folkways, institutional structures, ideologies and the fragments of ideologies that become enshrined in slogans, the power structure, the control of communications, sacred or treasured traditions, and genuine concern for people.

Usually there are conflicts within the ethic of a society. The traditional American ethic, for example, includes both admiration for rugged, competitive individualism and sympathy for the underdog. For many Americans the ethic includes both a reverence for the equality of men and a belief in white supremacy. When a decision involves a clash between two beliefs or two values, a society and the persons in it feel troubled. They may try to avoid a decision, or they may pretend that there is no clash. If events make the pretense impossible—as in the current American racial crisis—people feel pained or angry.

Decisions are especially hard to make in a time of major social change like the present. The old habits and traditions often do not fit the new situation. The traditions may not be worthless, but they seldom tell us what to do. Think of so simple an issue—if it is a simple one—as modesty in dress. We might compare women's bathing suits over the past century and notice the obvious changes. A woman would be ridiculous to apply her grandmother's standards of modesty to her own choice of a style. This does not mean that there is no such thing as modesty; it means only that expressions of modesty change. The grandmother would have been immodest if she had worn today's styles; today's woman is quaint rather than modest if she wears the styles of her grandmother's time.

In a time of change like our own we have real trouble in sorting out our values and making sound decisions. When past ideals are challenged, should we defend them or help to overthrow them? The question would often be difficult even if we had the best will in the world. Since we usually do not have the best will, the confusion grows worse. Everybody who stands to gain by the old ways is likely to call them God's will—whether the old ways be slavery, warfare, or denial that women and Negroes should vote. Everybody who sees the chance to make a fast dollar or to enjoy himself by taking a short cut is likely to decide that the old ethic is outmoded—whether it be honesty in business, marital fidelity, or mercy toward the weak.

People often yearn for general principles or standards of conduct that will not change, come what may. And of course there are general standards or qualities of character that are always fundamental. Trustworthiness, integrity, generosity, and compassion are not going to be outmoded by any new invention, social organization, or political program. But the meaning-in-action of these virtues does change. The generosity that once gave alms to the poor may now express itself in a program to give the poor man a job or to assure his family of medical care even though they cannot pay the bills. But as soon as I suggest these examples, I run into an area of controversy. That is to be expected. When ethical thinking sticks to generalities and avoids controversy, it is seldom important; as soon as it deals with live issues, it becomes controversial. And an era of social change like our own is bound to be an era of controversy.

Think of the time-honored commandment, "You shall love your neighbor as yourself." Ancient Judaism wrote the words into the book of Leviticus, and Jesus of Nazareth picked them out for special attention. Perhaps few people would want to argue against that commandment (although nobody finds it easy to obey). The commandment will not change because of anything that happens in Washington, at the United Nations, in our research laboratories, or in our industries. But no allegiance to the ancient commandment will tell us *exactly* and *directly* what it means for concrete action. It may mean actions that had never been thought of in biblical times: securing the neighbor's right to vote, enabling him to gain an education that no former generation could have enjoyed, assuring him that he will not lose employment because machines are taking over the jobs of men.

Responsible decisions today require an understanding of what is happening today. No loyalty to past standards can replace this contemporary knowledge. At the same time we must say that knowledge of the facts rarely dictates the decision. We still must determine what we will do with the facts. Our decision will rest upon our sensitivity to human needs, our deepest loyalties, our ultimate faiths.

The important decisions come at the meeting place between faith and facts. A belief in the worth of human persons is a faith. No laboratory, no electronic computer, no hypothesis of genetics, no invention will ever establish the faith. Some people will live and die by the faith, but not because facts have proved it. In some such way all the great beliefs are matters of faith. But the faith itself establishes no policies and dictates few decisions. Only when the faith meets hard facts—facts of juvenile delinquency, of racial hostility, of slums, of unemployment—do policies emerge. When faith meets facts, men must make decisions.

Often they prefer to avoid the issue or to stall; but refusal to act may be the most fateful action of all. A person can be murdered while spectators try to make up their minds whether to do anything; and a civilization can go to ruin while its citizens postpone the decisions that might save it.

Our own history is moving at a pace that perplexes us all. We have many opportunities to guide it. If we neglect the opportunities, the impersonal processes of history may take us to destinations that we shall regret.

The chapters that follow will take up successively some of the major areas in which the social changes of current history demand decisions. Each chapter will deal with open questions— with issues on which our society has not made up its mind, yet cannot avoid action. The chapters will describe aspects of contemporary life, analyze some of the processes that are going on, and point out issues that people today must meet.

2 | The Scientific Transformation of Life

OF ALL THE FORCES that are transforming our world none is more obvious than science. Our patterns of life are different from those of past generations because of the power of science. Future generations will live in ways that we can hardly guess—again because of science.

Living within a scientific revolution, we may scarcely realize how new and radical this powerful force is in human history. But the bare facts are startling. For example, it is estimated that of all the professional scientists who have lived on this earth, 90 per cent are now alive.[1] Or, to take another example, the United States government now spends on research and development more in one year than it spent for that purpose in the whole national history from the Revolutionary War until the end of World War II.[2]

Bertrand Russell has made the point in a different way. Man, he says, has existed for about one million years. He has known how to write for about 6,000 years. But science, "as a dominant factor in determining the beliefs of men," has been around for only about 300 years. And science as "a source of economic technique" has been available for only some 150 years.[3] Putting it another way, Lord Russell maintains: "One hundred and fifty years of science have proved more explosive than five thousand years of prescientific culture."[4] Russell chose that word "explosive" before the invention of nuclear weapons; the word has become far more apt than when he first used it.

SOME SOCIAL EFFECTS OF SCIENCE

The scientific revolution has reshaped the lives and prospects of people everywhere, including those who know very little about science. Let us look at a few ways in which science has restructured our own society.

First, there is work. Many people work at jobs that did not exist a century ago: air pilots, electronics engineers, automobile mechanics and salesmen, oil refiners and filling-station attendants. And all of us work at jobs that are vastly different from those we might have been doing 150 years ago.

The same science that makes new jobs destroys old jobs. Once a majority of people had to raise food in order that the

---

[1] Derek J. de Solla Price, *Science since Babylon* (New Haven, Conn.: Yale University Press, 1961), p. 107.

[2] Testimony of Dr. Jerome Wiesner, scientific adviser to the President, to a congressional committee. Reported in *Time*, Aug. 10, 1962.

[3] Bertrand Russell, *The Impact of Science upon Society* (New York: Simon and Schuster, 1953), p. 1.

[4] Bertrand Russell, *The Scientific Outlook* (New York: W. W. Norton, 1931), pp. vii-viii.

population might live. Now less than 10 per cent live on farms. Here is an estimate from Dr. Kenneth E. Boulding, the distinguished economist of the University of Michigan:

> It is by no means impossible to suppose a world at the end of this process in which we can produce our whole food supply with one per cent of the population; in which we can produce all basic commodities such as clothing, housing and so on with perhaps another two or three per cent or perhaps even at most ten per cent.[5]

We must wonder what the other 90 per cent will do. The forecast can be delightful or frightening.

Second, there is the revolution in transportation and communication. Every day people cross continents and oceans in a few hours. Satellites circle the earth several times a day. News travels with the speed of radio and telephone. As traffic jams get worse, it may take longer to cross town than it used to; but crossing the country has become a short trip.

In 1789, a messenger on horseback took seven days to take the news to George Washington of his election to the presidency. Now electronic computers and television tell people the results of elections before the polls are closed. Where once news required weeks to travel from Central Africa or Southeast Asia to Europe and America, now an angry word from an upstart dictator reverberates immediately in the major capitals of the world. Science has, for all practical purposes, changed the size and shape of the world.

Third, there is the contribution of science to health. All over the world life expectancy is increasing. Epidemics that once terrorized mankind have been wiped out with medicine and vaccines. Man has virtually conquered some diseases and is learning to conquer more. Surgery performs new miracles every year. We know more about healthful diets than ever before, and we have the resources to produce the necessary foods.

In skeptical moments we may suspect that the scientific advances in health barely enable us to keep up with the new diseases produced by a scientific society, especially the mental and emotional illnesses. But there is solid evidence of the basic accom-

[5] Kenneth E. Boulding, "The Death of the City: A Frightened Look at Post-Civilization," *Ekistics*, Jan., 1962.

plishment of medical science. One such evidence is the population explosion. A benefit of science that operates swiftly in impoverished countries is the reduction of infant mortality and the lengthening of the life span. As births increase and deaths are postponed, the population grows. We human beings are now increasing at a rate that will double the world's population in 35 or 40 years. If the present rate were to continue, in 600 years there would be only about one square yard of earth for each person in the world—and that counts all the deserts, mountains, and arctic lands. But we look to science, through increased food production and improved methods of birth control, to solve the problems it makes—if human beings are willing.

These are only a few of the social consequences of science. Other chapters of this book will deal with more. Anybody can add to the list from his own experience.

TWO FUNCTIONS OF SCIENCE

Now, instead of observing the social consequences of science, let us look at science itself to see something of how it operates. We can distinguish two functions of science: it gives us power to control our world (and maybe ourselves), and it gives us understanding.

The power to control is the more important function to most people. Often it outruns the ability to understand. Scientists themselves learned to use gravitation, magnetism, and electricity long before they understood them; in fact, we may ask even now whether they fully understand these phenomena. The nonscientist may understand very little of science or of the nature it studies, but he can enjoy its power to control. Rather few people understand exactly how an automobile operates; maybe nobody understands all the physical and chemical processes involved. But millions of people can drive a car. For every person who understands even vaguely how a television set works, there are thousands who can turn it on.

Knowledge is power, and power-hungry men seek knowledge. Because of scientific knowledge we can do all kinds of things that our ancestors could not do. Where they depended for their livelihood on the caprices of nature, we exploit nature for our purposes. Where they did things by muscle and sweat, we use machines.

Often our society has difficulty understanding the scientist with his love of research for its own sake. Society, including some of its political leaders, has distrusted, even persecuted, prominent nuclear physicists. It has scorned the "egg-head" and the "long-hair." But everybody appreciates more bang for a buck, more miles per gallon, more comfort for less work.

This power to control has significance for man's whole outlook upon himself and the world. All human living involves sometimes the spirit of manipulation, sometimes the spirit of acceptance. We manipulate, we control, we exercise power when we can. But some of the conditions of life are given. We can only accept them. If in much of history man has been impressed by the given nature of things, today he is impressed by what he can do. There is danger here: we may forget that life and death and the earth, our home, are given to us. There are powers we cannot manipulate. To ignore this truth is to lose the spirit of reverence and gratitude. But increasingly we can control things and events. This is wonderful too.

If the first achievement of science is power to control, the second achievement is understanding. Modern man has no more power to control an eclipse of the sun than had primitive man, who cowered in fear when the sun was darkened. But modern man is not afraid. Although he cannot hasten or postpone the eclipse by a single second, he knows when it will come. He dreams up no legends about dragons or evil spirits who darken the day. Instead he realizes that the moon crosses the face of the sun and blocks its light.

When Isaac Newton formulated the law of gravitation and gave a comprehensive theory of the action of all bodies in the universe, the poet Alexander Pope wrote:

> Nature and nature's laws lay hid in night,
> God said, "Let Newton be," and all was light.

Pope was exaggerating—wildly. He had no idea how many riddles lay beyond Newton's achievement. But he had an accurate sense of the way in which scientific understanding can dispel some of life's darkness. Knowledge, even without power to control, can cleanse us of superstition. It can remove many of life's fears.

The scientist has a love of knowledge that other men frequently cannot comprehend. The United States Congress will usually vote money for research that gives the power to control. It is more perplexed by the scientist's interest in pure knowledge of basic research. Why pay money to learn why grass is green? the politician or voter may ask. But science advances by asking questions that may lead to no practical results—or to great and often unexpected results.

To the scientist understanding may be more beautiful, more thrilling than manipulation. He loves to seek, to question, to learn. And his understanding infiltrates the entire society. Even those who do not share his sympathies find their attitudes changed because of the knowledge given them by science.

JOLTS FROM SCIENCE

Although science exalts man, by heightening his control and his understanding of the world, it also strikes blows against his self-esteem. Sometimes he seems to be reeling under these blows. Sigmund Freud has described a series of three jolts that modern science has delivered to man.[6]

Medieval man, says Freud (to paraphrase him roughly), saw himself as the crown of creation in the center of a universe that moved about him. Then Copernicus struck the first blow by showing man that he was not the center of everything. But man rallied and took comfort from the fact that, if he was not so important spatially, he was still a unique being, set off from the rest of nature. Next Darwin upset man with the second blow by showing him that he was a part of nature, descended from animals. That was harder to take, but again man rallied. He could still take satisfaction from his reason, which gave him a unique glory. Then, continues Freud, *I* came along and inflicted the third blow by showing man that he is not even rational.

[6] Sigmund Freud, *A General Introduction to Psychoanalysis* (Garden City, N.Y.: Garden City Publishing Co., 1943; first published, 1922), p. 252.

As Freud saw clearly, all this has been hard to take. To Freud's record we can add still another blow. The applied science or technology, which has increased man's powers in many ways, has simultaneously made him less sure about himself. Often he finds himself useless, as electronic devices take over functions that once only man could carry out—and perform them faster and with fewer mistakes. He fears also that his technology has wrought weapons that will destroy his civilization and himself.

In a later chapter I shall say something about man's self-understanding in this modern civilization. Here let us note what science has done to man's sense of his place in the universe. Once the universe was a wonderful and exciting place—mysterious, often frightening, but an authentic home, created by the same God who made man and showed his divine glory in all creation. Science, as many people have understood it, turns the universe into a blind, alien, purposeless mechanism. The poet Tennyson in the nineteenth century expressed in one line the shudder that many people felt:

> "The stars," she whispers, "blindly run." 7

Some people abandoned their traditional faith because of science. Others became hostile to science in order that they might cling to an old faith. Philosophies and historical movements, of which Marxism is the most influential, have sought to replace religion with science or pseudo-science.

Most of these conclusions have been entirely too glib and dogmatic. Religion is not adequate science, and science is not adequate religion. The scientific spirit and the religious spirit *can* live together and enrich each other. C. P. Snow, the agnostic scientist and novelist, has said:

Statistically, I suppose slightly more scientists are in religious terms unbelievers, compared with the rest of the world—though

---

7 *In Memoriam*, III. Alfred North Whitehead in his famous book, *Science and the Modern World* (New York: Macmillan, 1925), has commented on this line of Tennyson's and has argued that science now leads to a quite different conception of the world, in which purpose and beauty are as truly clues to the nature of things as are mechanisms.

there are plenty who are religious, and that seems to be increasingly so among the young.[8]

Harold K. Schilling, a physicist and a Christian, writes:

> Much of the Church, certainly as it is represented by its best minds, recognizes and takes into account all that is significant in modern science. I am aware of no established scientific discovery or conclusion which it rejects or proscribes; and there are many that it has appropriated for the clarification of its own understanding.[9]

This does not mean that it has been easy for modern man to bounce back from the jolting effect of science or to maintain both his scientific spirit and his religious faith. He can do so only if he is willing to give up the dogmatic spirit that so often plagues mankind.

As Dr. Schilling points out, there is developing "a discriminating, *reticent modesty* that makes us hesitate when tempted to claim *too* much for science." [10] Even so, he says, "Perhaps nowhere has science altered us more than in our religion." [11]

Certainly no one in a scientific society conceptualizes his faith in exactly the way that men of the past did. It may be, as many scholars have said, that the scientific spirit grows in part out of the biblical appreciation for the world and its order as God's creation. Even so, the most orthodox Christian sees his world and understands his beliefs in ways that would have been strange to the Apostle Paul, to Thomas Aquinas, or to Martin Luther. The most conservative Hindu departs in significant ways from the ideas of the Upanishads. Not only do men rethink their religious ideas; they bring their faith to new expressions and new decisions.

The jolts that science has brought to modern man have been brusque and sometimes painful. But man, if he is devoted to truth, need not fear them. If man lets science humble him with-

[8] C. P. Snow, *The Two Cultures and the Scientific Revolution* (New York: Cambridge University Press, 1959), p. 10.

[9] Harold K. Schilling, *Science and Religion: An Interpretation of Two Communities* (New York: Scribners, 1962), p. 2.

[10] Harold K. Schilling, "The Transforming Power of the Sciences," in *The Search for Identity: Essays on the American Character*, edited by Roger L. Shinn (New York: Harper & Row, 1964), p. 47.

[11] *Ibid.*, p. 52.

out humiliating him, lets it jar his beliefs without shattering his trustworthy convictions, he can reckon the discomforts of science among its benefits.

STILL HARDER DECISIONS AHEAD

All the signs indicate that science will be confronting us with decisions that are more perplexing than any we have faced yet. If we think of the importance of electricity, radio and television, and nuclear energy, we are likely to judge that, among the sciences, physics has brought the most portentous changes in recent years. But if we look ahead, we may guess that biology and biochemistry will have the most unsettling effect in the years to come.

We can expect that scientists will soon be producing life in laboratories. It will not be a very high grade of life. None of us will be picking his friends or marital partners from these laboratory products. But life with all its mystery will be removed—in part—from the realm of the given realities to the realm of human production. We cannot predict exactly what this will do for the "reverence for life" which has been so important to a man like Albert Schweitzer and which most of us feel at least to some degree.

Recent experiments have studied the workings of "consciousness-expanding drugs," which apparently have long been used in various forms by primitive tribes. The actual effect of these drugs is debatable: either they induce unusual, ecstatic experiences, or they free the subject from the inhibitions that normally prevent such experiences. Other drugs already in use can change a person's moods, and new drugs may change his personality traits. Surgical operations on the brain can modify a personality decisively. There are some speculations—far from confirmed —that the day is coming when a man can tell the doctor what kind of personality he would like to order, then get a prescription to fill the bill.

Still more puzzling are some of the recent developments in genetics. It is possible to modify the germ plasm, which is the physical bearer of our humanity from generation to generation. Parents, with the help of technicians, may someday predetermine the sex and many other traits of their children. No one knows how much can be done in this direction. It would be foolish to count on all the fanciful predictions that appear in the press. But in the light of the history of scientific achievements, it would also be foolish to set limits in advance to what science may find possible.

All these potentialities call for decisions. These decisions will be made gradually as research advances and people think over the possibilities. We human beings have a wise reluctance to experiment on ourselves and on one another. We count as one of the great crimes against the Nazis their readiness to let people—like inanimate objects or like rats—become the subject of experimentation that violated the dignity of personality. Yet the advance of medical science has always involved some element of experimentation with persons. The hesitation comes when the experiment concerns not simply some function of the organism but the personal being of man or woman.

We cannot settle these issues by a blanket rule against interfering with nature. After all, we constantly do that. An appendectomy, an injection of vaccine, even a bath might be called an interference with nature. All civilization is a modification of nature. But there are great dangers of rashness in the ambition of men, armed with scientific techniques, who are sure that they know what is good for others. Fallible man should be careful about irrevocable acts that mark other people, especially unborn children.

It is useless to try to answer in advance questions that have not yet come up for judgment. But now is the time to start thinking about possibilities that may stand on the close horizon. Some of these will test the greatest wisdom and ethical insight of man.

WHOSE DECISION?

It is part of the nature of human history that scientists, with all their powers, usually lack the power to decide what society will do with their scientific discoveries. This fact, often demonstrated in the past, presents an issue to scientists and to us all.

Recent world history offers dramatic evidence on this point. During World War II Albert Einstein alerted President Roosevelt to the possibility of making nuclear weapons. The peaceable Einstein did this because he feared that German scientists might make a bomb that Hitler could use for world conquest and destruction.

When the Allied forces invaded Europe, a special intelligence unit had the job of learning whether Germany was achieving an atomic bomb. At Strasbourg the Western forces captured German scientific papers. Professor Samuel Goudsmit, the chief scientific officer of the intelligence unit, examined the papers and discovered that Germany was not going to have the bomb any time soon. Later he commented to an army officer, "Isn't it wonderful that the Germans have no atom bomb? Now we won't have to use ours." The answer came back, "Of course you understand, Sam, if we have such a weapon, we are going to use it." As everybody knows, we did.

But many of the scientists working on the bomb had no such intention. Einstein himself said later, "If I had known that the Germans would not succeed in constructing the atom bomb, I would never have lifted a finger."[12]

The point is clear enough. Scientists give mankind new powers. Scientists alone do not decide what to do with these powers.

Who does decide? Society decides: individuals, governmental units, corporations, labor unions—all kinds of organizations decide. And they decide for many reasons: pride, fear, security, profit—these are some of the forces behind our decisions.

We do not always decide well. The world moves too fast, our purposes are divided, and we grow confused. James Reston puts it this way:

> In a restless, scientific society, we are all bewildered. All the relationships of the nation, region to region, Federal Government to state government, state to city, city to town, town to village and farm, employer to employee, white man to black man, and even

[12] For this entire episode see Robert C. Batchelder, *The Irreversible Decision: 1939–1950* (Boston: Houghton Mifflin, 1962), pp. 28-38.

parent to child—all these relationships have changed faster than human beings know how to change.[13]

There is one decision that we surely will not make. We will not, short of worldwide nuclear destruction, undo the scientific revolution. Occasionally somebody wishes we could. D. H. Lawrence, that self-consciously romantic novelist, had one of his characters say: "I'd wipe the machines off the face of the earth again, and end the industrial epoch absolutely, like a black mistake."[14] But that is plainly not about to happen. And it would not be right. The better and more courageous course is to use our science and industry—but to use them wisely.

The difficulty is that science and technology do not themselves tell us what to do with them. Bertrand Russell, skeptical though he is of all religions and all philosophies that are confident of right and wrong, has said clearly, "Whatever else may be mechanical, values are not." [15] If we feed data into electronic computers, we may get many answers, but we will not get moral judgments or solutions to our perplexities about values.

Perhaps we should be forgiven for our innocent confusions in an era when the motions of history are so swift and complicated. But our problems lie deeper even than innocent confusion. Albert Einstein once put the issue vividly: "It is easier to denature plutonium than to denature the evil spirit in man." At that point we must join to the achievements of science the concerns that prophets and poets have voiced through the centuries.

If individuals and groups support science primarily for the sake of private advantage and if governments subsidize research primarily for the sake of military might, we should not be surprised if science fails to deliver a better society. But man has a generous spirit as well as the evil spirit that Einstein noted. He is capable of seeking peace and the public good through science. When he questions the uses of science with the same rigorous determination that science employs in questioning nature, he is likely to find that science will serve him well.

[13] James Reston, column in *New York Times*, editorial page, May 29, 1964.
[14] D. H. Lawrence, *Lady Chatterly's Lover*, Chap. 15.
[15] Bertrand Russell, *The Impact of Science upon Society*, p. 60.

3 | The Affluent Society

IN RECENT YEARS a new phrase has entered the English—or perhaps I should say the American—language. The new phrase refers to a new fact: *the affluent society*. It goes with some other current phrases: the economy of abundance, the rich society, the age of high mass-consumption. Occasionally, more critical phrases have been used: the self-indulgent society, the overdeveloped nation, the economy of obsolescence, postcivilization. Call it what you will, it is an amazing phenomenon.

WHAT THIS SOCIETY IS LIKE

To describe it as briefly as possible, this is a society in which more people own, use, or consume more things than men ever did before or ever thought were possible before. Several countries have joined the affluent society, and more are on the way. The United States of America is the primary example.

The affluent society means, in the United States, that doctors more often warn people about eating too much than about eating too little. The nation has far more agricultural surpluses than shortages. Most people have the clothing they need, if not all they want. Americans have about 36 motor vehicles for every 100 persons. They have even more telephones than that. They have nearly as many radios as people—several per family, on average. There is a television set for every three persons, almost. Americans have learned the trick of producing more and more things with fewer man-hours of work.

At the very beginning we must notice one paradox in the affluent society. Most people do not consider themselves rich. A

25

majority are straining hard to get along. Very few have all that they want.

One reason for this is that most people want a lot. Among other things, most of us would like to have a little more than the people around us. And nobody has figured out how most people can have more than the people around them.

Another reason is that it is almost impossible to live and function in the affluent society without having a lot. The illustrations of the fact are everywhere. For most of the world's three billions of people an automobile is an almost incredible luxury. In the affluent society many a person cannot earn a living without one, and the economy would strangle without millions of them. As for housing, past generations and much of present mankind would consider central heating, elaborate plumbing, electric lights and refrigeration, and elevators to be impressive luxuries. In the affluent society a city would die in its filth and confusion if it lost these. The former luxuries have become basic necessities for many, many people.

The opposite side of the story is that some of the simple pleasures of life, which people have enjoyed with no cost for centuries, have become expensive luxuries. People who want to breathe fresh air, go fishing, look at the stars, or take a walk in the countryside often go to frantic efforts for the sake of these enjoyments.

For several reasons, therefore, the family in the affluent society may feel a greater economic strain than its ancestors in far poorer societies. Man seldom achieves solid gains that do not involve new problems.

If the affluent society does not put everybody on the easy trail, we can nevertheless describe it in terms of several characteristics that affect everybody. Let us look at three of these.

1. The economy produces a tremendous quantity of goods and—equally important—distributes them among the vast majority of its people. Starvation, the ancient enemy of man, no longer need threaten him. There are more than enough clothes for everybody. There is a place for everybody to come in out of the rain or the cold. When people lack good food, clothing, and housing, it is not for the traditional reason that the society can-

not produce enough. We can produce plenty. Although we still have to learn how to distribute our goods to everybody, we do manage to get them to most people. The average person, not just the privileged, enjoys the necessities of life and something more.

2. In order to keep the wheels of industry rolling, society tries a variety of techniques to stimulate consumption. Government designs tax policies to encourage people to spend money. Editorials tell us that it is our duty to spend. And above all, we advertise. Advertising is so common a part of our life that we seldom stop to think what an amazing phenomenon it is. Here is a vast industry whose purpose is not to produce but to persuade people to consume. To the people in the first million years of human history the present function of advertising would be unbelievable. For most of the human race scarcity has been the great problem; there just was not enough to go around. Now a society has so much that it thinks up new ways of tempting people to consume. If people restrain themselves, the economy slows down and everybody suffers.

3. Work, as we began to see in the last chapter, is not what it used to be. Fewer and fewer people earn their living by the sweat of the brow, and those who do so work for shorter hours. Possibly more people earn a living by the strain on their nerves. The style of work is changing. Technology takes away old jobs and makes new ones. Sometime in the 1950s the United States passed an epochal turning point in history—and hardly anybody noticed it. Nothing like it had ever happened to any large society. The number of white-collar workers passed the number of blue-collar workers. This does not mean that white-collar workers are more important than blue-collar workers; it means only that there are more of them. It takes fewer people to work the farms, manufacture goods, and haul them around than to do the planning, the paper work, and the selling. We have looked at Kenneth E. Boulding's prediction about the future (p. 15 above). The current facts and the outlook mean a change in the whole mood of society, in education, in the expectations of the young.

We could note other characteristics of the affluent society, but these three give us enough to think about. They make it evident that this way of living offers opportunities and raises questions that the human race has never before faced in quite the same way.

THE BLESSINGS OF ABUNDANCE

Nobody has to argue that a good meal is better than starvation, and no pollster has to ask the public whether it prefers prosperity or poverty. All of us enjoy the variety of foods in the supermarket. We like to sit down in the evening and choose from the educational or entertaining programs on television. We like to drive cars and travel in planes. We like to take vacations.

Beyond such obvious enjoyments there are substantial values in the affluent society. We can learn to appreciate them. It is foolish to hide them by using the common slogans that praise spiritual values and deplore material values. In human life the spiritual and the material are intertwined. (The Bible, we may note, says far more about food, rent, money, debts, and work than many people realize.) We can point to several ways in which material wealth contributes to the genuine well-being of humanity.

First, a productive economy makes possible the practical expression of concern for persons. It is difficult—not impossible but difficult—to believe in the importance of every person and to carry that belief into practice in a world where epidemics and starvation waste life. A high standard of living makes possible opportunities for everybody. Social security, for example, with its protection against unemployment and old age, is possible only in a society that has at least moderate prosperity. We should note that some societies less wealthy than our own do more than we along this line; but unemployment insurance and widespread retirement plans are not a live option in a society like India's.

One of the benefits of science, we noted earlier, is its contribution to health. The research that improves health is costly, as is medical care and hospitalization. Our affluent society has brought advantages in health to many people, and it can learn to do much more than it has yet done.

A second gain is in education. In times when most people *had* to perform physical labor most of the time, few people could gain a rich education. They might acquire a practical wisdom in doing the job and learning to live with other people, but they could not learn much about the world beyond their immediate ken.

By making education widely available, our productive economy has a democratic effect. Plato and Aristotle believed that "the good life" was possible only for a few people. Slaves and artisans, as well as women, could not attain true happiness and should not be citizens. Along with the snobbery in this attitude was a hard-headed realization of some facts: few people had access to education or even to elementary political information. If a man could spend his time in the market place talking to Socrates and his fellow citizens, he could learn enough to vote wisely. But if he had to work for a living, he would not understand the political issues. Today any worker on a 40-hour week can, if he makes the effort, get a comprehensive political education from newspapers, magazines, radio, television, and low-priced books.

Our society can urge and require children to stay in school, at least until they are sixteen, rather than stopping school to go to work. As a matter of fact, as far as the economy is concerned, we can afford to let anybody who wishes go to school until he is twenty-one or twenty-five. Not every person or family can afford that kind of education, but the society can make it possible any time it decides to do so.

A third and closely related gain is leisure. Some of the gains in leisure are an illusion; many people never have time to do what they want. The shorter working day is not much help to people who spend hours fighting traffic jams to get to work. The longer weekend gives little relaxation if the family spends half the time soaking up carbon monoxide in order to enjoy fresh air for the other half. Furthermore, leisure brings its problems. The world is full of people who are bored with the effort to amuse themselves in their idle time. We can grant all these difficulties and still appreciate the blessings of leisure.

The high culture of most past civilizations has depended largely upon a small leisure class. A few people had enough time and freedom from other work to write novels and read them, to form symphony orchestras and listen to them. We can only guess at the number of potential geniuses whose talents could never flower because of the burden of work—even as we admire those who overcame adversity. Today we have the possibility, already partly realized, of admitting our whole society to the leisure class.

In several ways, it is evident, economic affluence can improve the quality of life. It makes possible not simply an easier life but the realization of many human potentialities. Along with these gains, it poses its threats and dangers.

CHALLENGES OF PROSPERITY

Two problems in this affluence are so big and so urgent that I shall defer them for special emphasis later. One is the persistence of intolerable poverty within the richest society the world has ever known; that will be the topic of Chapter 4. The other is the relation of prosperous countries to a desperately poor world; that will receive attention in Chapter 10. Here we shall look at some of the ways in which wealth and the use of wealth bring challenges to our civilization.

First we may note that the affluent economy often manages to thrive by appealing to the worst motives of people rather than to their best. The furious flow of products from the factories brings a perverse pressure on people to buy and consume. Carl Sandburg, worried on this count, said to a newspaper man: "When the goal of a country is only happiness and comfort, there is danger. . . . All these things in the advertisements—any time the main goal of life is to get them, so that they override your other motives, there's danger."

How serious is this danger? One way to investigate is to pick up any popular magazine and study the advertisements. The point is not to theorize about advertising: we can quickly grant that, like most human activities, it has both useful and harmful social functions. Instead we can examine the actual advertising layouts and discover what motives they exploit. Thousands of readers have learned from Vance Packard in *The Hidden Persuaders* about the "motivational research," which enables the advertiser to "sneak up" on the blind side of people and work on motives that the consumers do not recognize or understand.

Arnold Toynbee, the world-famous historian, has these harsh things to say about advertising:

> It has made a fine art out of taking advantage of human silliness. It rams unwanted goods down surfeited throats when two-thirds of all human beings now alive are in desperate need of the bare necessities of life. This is an ugly aspect of the affluent society; and, if I am told that advertising is the price of affluence, I reply without hesitation, that affluence has been bought too dear.[1]

Nobody has to accept the conclusions of Vance Packard or of Arnold Toynbee. Anybody can make his own investigation. In any typical collection of advertisements he can find appeals to pride, envy, snobbery, sexual dominance, conformity, will to power, fallacious security, self-indulgence. He can also find appeals to family loyalty, intellectual awareness, generosity. He can find art that degrades and art that elevates public taste. He can find anything he is looking for, but he will find plenty to justify some worries.

The answer is not to imitate Thoreau and hunt for a Walden Pond where one can live the good, simple life. Finding the Walden Pond will itself be a problem; with the present population of America there are not enough ponds to go around, and the realtors are promoting most of those that there are. Furthermore Thoreau never realized how much he depended upon the civilization that he criticized. But Thoreau still asks troubling questions about our aims and motives.

An earlier American than Thoreau questions us in a different way. John Woolman, the eighteenth-century Quaker who protested against slavery and exploitation of labor, became concerned about his own success as a retail merchant. He wrote in his *Journal*: "I found it good for me to advise poor people to take such things as were most useful, and not costly." A modern Woolman would occupy a strange place in society. Probably people would think him queer—and, indeed, some persons so regarded Woolman. They might further consider him a traitor to the American spirit of initiative and ambition.

Times have changed since Woolman and Thoreau. While

---

[1] Arnold Toynbee, "Why I Dislike Western Civilization," *New York Times Magazine* (May 10, 1964), p. 30.

we can learn from them, we must also learn to live in a world they never saw. There are valuable achievements and more valuable potentialities in our affluent society, as I have already argued. But the values are constantly threatened by the frantic pressures to buy and to consume.

That brings us to a *second* challenge from the affluent economy. There is not the slightest doubt that high productivity and consumption undermine some of the old-fashioned virtues. Maybe these virtues ought to be abandoned and replaced by new ones. Even so, the possible changeover is apt to cause uneasiness.

The discussion goes on in big debates about federal expenditures and fiscal policies. It also goes on in little debates in the family. Parents wonder whether things come too easily for the children. And children, if they hear how parents once worked for ice cream cones or put nickels in school savings accounts, ask whether Mom and Dad were born in the Middle Ages.

Much of the ethic of the past has been built on the assumption of scarcity. Since there were never enough consumer goods, duty called for restraint. Copybooks in school and sermons in church emphasized the virtues of hard work, of frugality, of avoiding waste, of saving for a rainy day. The conscientious person lived within a set of disciplines that forbade extravagance, self-indulgence, and debt for any reason except grave emergency.

The affluent society invites us to throw off most of those disciplines. It tells us that we can have our cake and eat it too, via the installment plan. If we resist the new rules, we not only miss a lot of fun; we also are guilty of contributing to unemployment. The economy encourages waste: why save food when the government is storing huge farm surpluses, and why fix up the old appliance when repairs cost as much as a new model?

Most of us are likely to be a little less loyal to the traditional virtues than our parents, a little more loyal than our children—and thoroughly confused. Almost any political candidate can cash in on an appeal to those virtues, and some of them make a career of it. We may not practice the rules that Benjamin Franklin set down—as he himself often neglected to practice them—but they have an almost religious appeal to many Americans.

As a matter of fact, the appeal definitely is religious, because these virtues became associated with Christianity at one stage of its history. To criticize them makes many people feel unfaithful —even though Christian faith in its origins had little to do with some of these virtues. The issue today is to distinguish between those practices that have a continuing importance for life and faith, and those practices that once became temporarily associated with faith.

A good example is the relation between work and relaxation. David Riesman in a famous book has written: "The inner-directed person, if influenced by Protestantism, is . . . unable to waste time."[2] If that is an exaggeration, let's say he is uncomfortable about wasting time. If he is old enough, he was once taught, "Satan finds work for idle hands to do." The word "Satan" gives the proverb a religious quality. But Satan in the Bible works differently. From the Bible one would suppose that relaxation and contemplation are as fundamental to life as feverish work and that Satan finds especially vulnerable targets in ambitious competitors.

Our ancestors were not wrong in recognizing the importance of a disciplined life. But the disciplines that were truly important to them are not necessarily the disciplines that are most important to us. We can enjoy the pleasure of escaping some old disciplines with good conscience—provided we are willing to undertake new ones. And that is harder to do.

The effort to revise the traditional disciplines brings us to a *third* challenge. Even an affluent society must make choices. It cannot do everything. It must select priorities and allot its resources. Some of these decisions pinch.

The phrase, "the affluent society," gained wide usage from Galbraith's book by that same name.[3] Galbraith, a Harvard economist, maintains that the United States pampers the private sector of its economy and starves the public sector. At first glance anybody, looking at his own tax bill and the size of the governmental budgets, is likely to argue with Galbraith. But a great

---

[2] David Riesman, *et al., The Lonely Crowd* (Garden City, N.Y.: Doubleday Anchor Book, 1953; first published, 1950), p. 184.

[3] John Kenneth Galbraith, *The Affluent Society* (Boston: Houghton Mifflin, 1958).

part of taxation—well over half of the federal budget—goes to military expenses. It is the remaining part, which goes for general public services, that has not kept pace with the growth of our society.

Here are two examples. (1) Surveying the last two decades, economist James W. Kuhn of Columbia University writes: "Wealthier than ever before, Americans have held down or actually decreased the share of income used by their government to aid the sick and to comfort the poor."[4] The share of America's whole income (Gross National Product) which has gone into federal government expenditures, apart from defense, has fallen since the period before World War II. (2) Looking at local school budgets, we find that Americans were spending more per pupil (allowing for the changing value of the dollar) in 1900 than they are six decades later.

Probably all of us have natural reluctance to pay more into the public sector of the economy. We enjoy buying things personally more than we enjoy buying them with other people through our governments. When our children are in public schools, we may feel the urgency of improving the quality of education. As soon as they get out of school, we have stronger feelings about trading in the car than about the schools—even though we still approve good schools on principle. We would rather buy a new television set than pay for slum rehabilitation, unless we happen to be living in the slums. If we have pleasant homes in the suburbs, we are not inclined to have our taxes go to solving problems of the city, even though our personal economic welfare depends largely on the cities. Above all, we prefer consuming goods ourselves rather than building up the economy of South America or India.

Furthermore the government can more easily get appropriations for emergencies than for the basic programs that could prevent emergencies. If there is a wave of crime or juvenile delinquency, people will clamor for more police before they will pay the money to get at the causes of trouble. The public tolerates

---

[4] James W. Kuhn, *et al.*, *Christians Face Issues of High Moment in Our Changing Economy* (New York: National Council of Churches, 1962), p. 22. The data in the rest of the paragraph above come from this same source.

incredibly bad schools without much complaint. It allows pollution of air and water, degeneration of public transportation, inadequate sanitation. The most influential people can often afford to avoid these sore spots in society, and usually they would rather do so than pay the bills to correct them.

I do not want to imply that any of these problems can be solved by money alone. A commercial society is too ready to think that it can buy solutions to every ailment. The needs of American society call for the best scientific skills and ethical imaginations—and for money. Although money alone cannot solve the problems, they cannot be solved without money.

Let us turn to a *fourth* challenge before the affluent society. This society is wealthy largely because it is adaptable. Its quick changes make old skills obsolete and hurt some people as other people gain. Often a person finds with suddenness that the abilities which earned him a living are no longer useful.

The most obvious case is farming. The successful farmer with his scientific methods produces more and more. Hence society needs fewer farmers. The number of farms in the United States decreased by 1.5 million in the 1950s. Now 1.5 million farmers turn out 87 per cent of America's agricultural produce. Two million farmers raise the remaining 13 per cent. The 1.5 million could without much trouble do the whole job, making the 2 million expendable. We can with relative ease write off the 2 million marginal farms—but not the farmers. They are human beings whose skills are no longer needed.

The same problem overtakes some men with far greater technical skills. Peter F. Drucker has described the case of the flight engineer, whose span of usefulness ran for about 15 years. His job became necessary when the multi-engined piston planes came to dominate the airways. He was not wanted when jets replaced the pistons. The well-paid, highly skilled man suddenly wondered what useful ability he had. The affluent society, which is greatly concerned about skills, must decide how it will express its concern about persons.

A *fifth* challenge to the affluent society—the last we shall consider—is a more general one, which follows from the others. It affects the way a person thinks of himself, of his neighbors, of his world. It influences us in both obvious and subtle ways. It is not easy to describe, but we might sum it up in a sentence. Man-the-producer tends to become man-the-consumer. The producer is still necessary. But increasingly machines do both the manual labor and the clerical work of production. A great many people —the 2 million farmers we just noticed and comparable men in railroads, on docks, and in factories—are not needed as producers. They remain important as consumers. The affluent society will not entirely forget them—partly because these people have ways of reminding us of their presence, partly because the whole economy drags when they stop spending, partly because the affluent society still has a conscience.

Man cannot survive without consuming. He can survive without producing. Society needs producers for its survival, but does not need as many as it used to need. Idle rich and idle poor remain consumers. And the whole atmosphere of the society comes to emphasize the gratifications of consumption more than of production. If Freud was right—that the important abilities of man are to love and to work—we may dehumanize ourselves by making work unimportant.

The elaborate division of labor contributes to the same effect. The village blacksmith knew what he produced. Every day he could see his products around town. His grandson, working on an assembly line in a factory, does not actually produce any tangible object. He has a minute part to do with the production of many things. But he does not follow the objects of his work to the end of the line. He does not recognize his own work as he drives home. It is not surprising that he often takes more pride in a do-it-yourself accomplishment around the house than in the job at the factory.

In part we shall simply have to learn to live with these changes, substituting new satisfactions for old ones. In part we shall discover better ways of relating work to men. In part we shall gradually learn to redefine production and useful work. We have always recognized that a man, making an object to be trucked to a store and sold, is a producer. We have been less ready to recognize that a nurse, an artist, a teacher, a student are producers. The time may come when, instead of asking a student to pay for his higher education, we shall decide to pay him, as we pay workers in factories and offices. In fact, we have begun to do this through various types of scholarships and subsidies. The college undergraduate playing big-time football or the graduate student doing research in nuclear physics may be rather well rewarded. Our society may decide to extend the system and adjust the inequities in it. An affluent society can afford to do so; and if it wants to, it can invent the techniques.

A QUESTIONING HOPE

We have looked at some of the blessings and some of the challenges of the affluent society. For most of us most of the time the advantages are self-evident. Affluence is a problem only because we want more of it. We cannot imagine a candidate running for the presidency of the United States—or of a corporation or a trade union—on an anti-affluence platform. Growth, rising standard of living, comfort, security—these are usually uncriticized goods.

Occasionally some critic dares to question the assumption that *more* and *faster* are always *better*. He may throw into doubt the whole nature of the high-powered and rich society. Although he rarely convinces people completely, he usually awakens some response. Enough people talk about the rat-race, the merry-go-round, and the treadmill to make it evident that there is considerable uneasiness about this way of life.

The questioning is right, provided it does not cause us to turn our backs on the opportunities before us. The opportunities are authentic. And we have a better chance to realize them if we question them both relentlessly and hopefully.

D. L. Munby, the British economist, has written a book called *God and the Rich Society*. In it he uses language that is unusual for an economist: "God is in process of transforming our economic order. . . . We can, and should, participate in that activity."[5] The statement may make us think of Dietrich Bonhoeffer, who in concentration camp shortly before he was murdered by the Nazis called for a Christian worldliness. These men

[5] D. L. Munby, *God and the Rich Society* (London: Oxford University Press, 1961), p. 179.

are saying that authentic faith leads us not to withdraw from the world but to participate in it to the full.

But then what? How shall we tell the difference between valid worldliness and heedless worldliness? How shall we distinguish between the workings of God in our economic order and the workings of sordid ambition and blind greed? One way is to question our society, to seek to discover how and why decisions are made, and to learn what the social process is doing to people.

Such acts, important in any society, have a special and specific importance in our own. The dynamics of an affluent society seem to acquire a momentum and direction of their own. The processes—like the automated machinery within them—operate almost as though nobody were directing them. Obviously people keep making decisions for reasons that look good to them. But the impersonal system, acting like an invisible board of directors, settles a lot of questions.

Notice what happens when an electronic machine replaces men in a job. (I am not saying this should never happen. I am only looking into the way in which it happens.) Every act of automation and every replacement of men by machines is obviously the decision of some person or committee. But usually the individual decision is practically inevitable. Competitors are doing it, progress calls for it, the corporation has to do it or lose business and dwindle away. So the system really makes the decision. And if we ask who has looked at the system and evaluated the gains and losses involved, we do not find any easy answer.

Economist Robert L. Heilbroner has stated well the fateful quality of the system: "It is not mere rhetoric to ask if Things are not already in the saddle riding Man. . . . Man will surely never ride Things unless he is prepared to ask questions which today do not often seem to occur to him."[6]

The asking of those questions becomes an urgent task of the affluent society. For what purposes shall we use our new powers? How shall we make their benefits available to all? How can we control the forces of our own creation? Does the welfare of the

[6] Robert L. Heilbroner, "The Impact of Technology: The Historic Debate," in *Automation and Technological Change*, edited by John T. Dunlop (Englewood Cliffs, N.J.: Prentice-Hall, 1962), pp. 7, 25.

system override the welfare of the people in it? How can decisions be made responsibly in our kind of world?

As it deals with such questions this rich, powerful society will be driven to the ancient question: "For what will it profit a man, if he gains the whole world and forfeits his life?" (Matt. 16:26.)

4 | Poverty in the Midst of Plenty

THE RICHEST SOCIETY in the world—in fact, the richest society in all history—includes desperate poverty. This society, as we have seen, turns out vast quantities of consumer goods and distributes them widely among its members. But at the bottom of the heap are those who get left out.

Line up 100 "average" Americans. About 80 of them belong, more or less, to the affluent society. Most of the 80, for reasons we have noticed, strain to balance their budgets. Most of them hanker after products they cannot buy. But they contribute to the prodigious consumption of this economy. The 20 poorest are painfully poor. They are migrants, marginal farmers, city slum-dwellers. Four of them are Negroes. Society dangles before them its advertisements, its goods, its invitations to spend. These people look at the alluring goods as strangers. They do not belong or expect to belong.

CONTRASTS

Often poverty persists in the shadow of wealth. Such is the case in the major American cities. The situation of many cities becomes dramatically visible on one street of the biggest city: Park Avenue in New York.

Park Avenue starts at midtown, where the giant new Pan-American building rises for 59 stories above Grand Central Station. Immediately north of it are the great office buildings, erected in metal and glass since World War II. The most notable among them—the House of Seagram and Lever House—combine mass and space in an exhilarating way. They tell of wealth, efficiency, and imagination—not the imagination that built Gothic cathedrals or wrote Shakespeare's plays, but a modern imagination, the imagination of an industrial society that knows how to use machines, how to produce wealth, and still appreciates beauty.

Most of the buildings lining the street represent industry, banking, retailing, stockbrokers, and the church. In the crowded street limousines, competing for space with taxis and ordinary automobiles, draw up to the Waldorf-Astoria Hotel and to the office buildings. Usually the sidewalks are filled with people, most of them prosperous and well dressed. The skins are of all colors, but mostly white. Walking along the street and glancing at the window displays, no one would be likely to guess that the metropolis houses more rats than people. Although the rat census is not guaranteed for strict accuracy, the estimate is that one million more rats than people live in this city.

To the north the street becomes residential. Here is an area of luxurious apartment houses, of doctors' offices, of occasional hotels. In lavish churches the worshipers sometimes hear bold sermons that appeal to their social conscience. At Hunter College gifted young people get high-quality education free.

Farther northward the buildings gradually become more modest. This is not the dazzling wealth of the downtown area. This is normally prosperous America. The prosperity continues for a while—then stops as abruptly as if a Berlin wall blocked the street.

But there is no wall. The major change is the railroad. The New York Central tracks have been running underground beneath a beautiful green strip in the middle of the avenue. At 96th Street they emerge into an elevated railroad that marks the whole neighborhood with its noise and shadow. Here both sides of the railroad are the wrong side of the tracks. This is still Park Avenue, but no longer the legendary Park Avenue. This is Harlem.

The street has changed from smooth asphalt to bumpy brick. The people have changed too. Most of them are dark-skinned. Some of them wear clothes less costly than the pet dogs wear farther downtown. The people walk by dark tenements, unbearably hot in the summer, often cold in the winter. They walk past an occasional housing project, a dreary school, count-less stores, and more dark tenements. The signs in store windows or on the sides of buildings are in Spanish as often as English. Inside the shops and the street stalls is as much variety as in the specialty shops downtown, but nobody can miss seeing the difference. The customers are mostly Negroes and Latin Ameri-cans. The owners are mostly white. Custom and the economic structure decree that Negroes rarely own businesses.

Children play in crowded, dirty streets. Vacant spaces be-come not handsome plazas like those downtown but places for a collection of debris. Peddlers pull rickety handcarts to a junk-store, where they unload the day's collection from streets and refuse bins around town. They make their living from the waste in an affluent society.

The area is dotted with churches. Some congregations meet in modest, conventional church buildings and carry out a special ministry to children. Others gather in store-fronts. The usual denominations, familiar all over America, are here. So are the Pentecostalists and various sects and independent movements. All acknowledge Jesus Christ. The members are brothers under God to the members of ornate churches downtown, but they have little relationship to each other on Park Avenue.

The avenue ends at the Department of Welfare on the Har-lem River. Here people collect the payments that enable them to survive in the affluent society. Most of them seem to be mothers. Often they bring their little children with them or park their babies in the buggies by the door while they go inside.

The persons who get help here are part of about 8 million Americans who live on relief. Despite the growing wealth and production, the number on relief has been growing. From 1955 to 1964 it grew about twice as fast as the population.[1]

The story of Park Avenue is not unique. Not every city has a

[1] *Newsweek* (Feb. 17, 1964), p. 19.

single street which starts as a showcase to the world and ends with the Department of Welfare. But every major city has residents who enjoy lavish wealth and those who survive in dismal poverty.

DISCOVERY

Brutal poverty is for most Americans a recent discovery. During the Great Depression starting in 1929 everybody knew about poverty. Although America pulled out of that depression during the New Deal, people often forget that real prosperity was not attained until the years of war production. Since then Americans have been more or less in a war economy, with tremendous military expenditures. Production has been high and, except for minor recessions, the country has been prosperous.

Since most people shared in the prosperity, they paid little attention to persisting poverty. Those who owned newspapers and wrote for them, those who controlled radio-television and did the broadcasting, those who were active in politics, the members of middle-class churches—all those shared in the prosperity. The poor had few means of communication. The affluent society almost forgot them.

Then came the discovery of poverty in America. A series of books and magazine articles told the story.[2] Some of the poor, especially in racially deprived groups, organized and made themselves heard. Several political leaders took up the cause of the poor. The discovery has shaken American society enough that citizens may now do something about it.

No attempt to measure poverty can be entirely exact, because it is hard to draw the line between the really poor and the many who think they need more than they have. For practical

[2] See Michael Harrington, *The Other America: Poverty in the United States* (New York: Macmillan, 1963; also a Penguin paperback). Gabriel Koko, *Wealth and Power in America* (New York: Praeger, 1963). James N. Morgan, *et al.*, *Income and Welfare in the United States* (New York: McGraw-Hill, 1962). Herman P. Miller, *Rich Man, Poor Man* (New York: Crowell, 1964). Edgar May, *The Wasted Americans* (New York: Harper & Row, 1964). Ben H. Bagdikian, "The Invisible Americans," *Saturday Evening Post*, Dec. 21-28, 1963. Douglass Cater, "The Politics of Poverty," *The Reporter*, Feb. 13, 1964. *Newsweek*, Feb. 17, 1964. The basic data which I use in this chapter are given in most of these sources.

purposes the usual boundary line is set at a family income of $3,-000 per year. Most studies by governmental and private agencies indicate that the average family of four needs $5,000 or $6,000 a year to manage moderately well, so the figure of $3,000 is hardly too high. The families with less than $3,000 a year *know* they are poor.

Of course, it is possible to argue with any figure. A married student and wife, whose housing is partly subsidized and who can use the college health service, may be comfortable at $3,000 a year until the babies start coming. Or a retired couple who own their home, do not need a car, and have some savings may live on less than $3,000 of income, barring serious illness. On the other hand, a family of four to six persons, living in a city, will feel the hurt of poverty if they make $4,000 a year. So if we go along with the usual figure of $3,000, we are certainly not being too generous.

With this yardstick we find that 1 family out of 5 in this country lives in severe poverty. This lowest fifth (more than 9 million families) get less than $3,000 a year. More than half of them receive less than $2,000 a year. The lowest 20 per cent of American people have to get along on 5 per cent of America's income.

This lowest fifth are not the people who feel poor because they have to keep the car another year before trading for a new one. They are not the thousands who are sorry for themselves because they have to eat hamburger instead of T-bone steaks. They are people in wretched shacks or slums which they cannot keep clean by any trying. They do not have enough to eat or a diet to sustain health. They rarely see a doctor or a dentist. They do not make plans for next year.

The President's Council of Economic Advisers in 1964 used these words to describe the world of the poor:

> It is a world apart, whose inhabitants are isolated from the mainstream of American life and alienated from its values. It is a world where Americans are literally concerned with day-to-day survival—a roof over their heads, where the next meal is coming from. It is a world where a minor illness is a major tragedy, where pride and privacy must be sacrificed to get help, where honesty can

become a luxury and ambition a myth. Worst of all, the poverty of the fathers is visited upon the children.[3]

For a long time Americans have enjoyed the illusion that they were narrowing the gap between wealth and poverty. Actually they are not. For a while they were. Between 1929 and 1944 the wealthiest fifth of the population dropped in its share of the income, while the remainder of the population gained. Even then the lowest fifth improved only slightly. In the next 20 years the gap did not change at all.[4] This is not to argue that it is possible or good to *eliminate* the gap. But the fact is that the gap between rich and poor is a great one and there should be no pretense that it is being reduced when actually it is not.

WHO ARE THE POOR?

When we locate the poor in American society, we find that they are a diverse group. There is no one cause of poverty; hence there is no one cure.

One way of classifying the desperately poor puts them in four groups: the unemployed, marginal farmers, unskilled workers, and the aged. A variety of causes and possible remedies enter into the picture in each case.

1. The unemployed have an obvious reason to be poor. As a matter of fact, most of the poor are not unemployed, but some of them certainly are. There are several reasons for unemployment. Some workers are laid off whenever production is low. Some lack the skills that would get them jobs, either because they never learned a skill or because machines have made their skills useless. Some live in areas—Appalachia is the best known—where there is chronic shortage of work.

2. As we saw in Chapter 3, the United States has many more farmers than it needs. Some of these are sharecroppers and tenant farmers. Some own small, uneconomic farms. Some are migrant workers, who are needed only seasonally. Obviously some of these farmers will eventually quit farming and find jobs elsewhere—or

[3] *New York Times,* Jan. 21, 1964.
[4] Herman P. Miller (of the U.S. Bureau of the Census), "Is the Income Gap Closed? 'No!' " *New York Times Magazine,* Nov. 11, 1962. Also columnist TRB, *The New Republic,* Apr. 4, 1964.

if they do not, their children will. But often farming is the only job they know. They can continue in wretched farm poverty or move to city slums and get used to the equally wretched poverty of the unemployed.

3. There are about 7 million unskilled workers who receive a little pay most weeks of the year but not enough to support a family. Some of these are illiterate. Some are women working heroically to support a family. These workers find jobs not covered by the minimum wage laws. If somebody earns one dollar an hour—and many earn less—he can put in a 40-hour week throughout the year and earn only $2,080. When work is irregular, he makes less.

4. The aged are often poor. Improved pension plans and social security benefits are helping people to retire without suffering. But some 8 million live in poverty. Some of these never were able to plan for their old age. Others planned, but their plans could not meet bad health or the rising cost of living.

These four classifications include most of the Americans who are badly hurt by poverty. In each group are some who suffer especially because of racial problems. About one-half million American Indians live in squalid poverty, as do some Spanish Americans and other ethnic groups. Negroes make up the group that bears the worst brunt of poverty. Negro unemployment is twice as high as white unemployment, and Negro pay averages 40 per cent less than white. America has taken tardy steps to secure civil rights for its Negro citizens. But these gains will not amount to much unless Negroes can enter freely into economic processes with equal opportunity to work, to gain promotion, and to secure capital and real estate so that they can operate businesses.

Since poverty has so many complex causes, no single solution will be enough. The answer to intolerable poverty will include many efforts.

1. We need more jobs. The usual estimate is 25,000 new jobs per week for the next 10 years. That will not simply happen without any planning. Nor will prosperity automatically provide that many jobs. Some will come through economic growth. Others will come through redistributing work by methods often used in the past: prolonged education so that youths do not seek

work so soon, earlier retirement for older workers, shorter hours, more vacations. Still more may come through reconceiving the nature of work, as suggested in the preceding chapter.

2. Special efforts are necessary for areas where employment has fallen. Either people must be moved out or jobs must be moved in.

3. We must improve education and the incentives for young people to go to school. If we investigate the poorest fifth of the American population, we find that in a majority of cases the head of the family has not finished high school. In 35 per cent of the cases the head of the family has not even entered high school.[5] With the current rate of high school dropouts (40 per cent) Americans are building poverty for the future.

4. We must solve the race problem with its intolerable consequences for human misery. At present we are involved in a vicious circle. The white worker fears and resents the Negro, whom he sees as a threat to his job. He can scarcely overcome this prejudice until the economic situation improves for both Negro and white. Yet the Negro cannot improve his economic situation until prejudice declines. The circle has to be broken from both sides—i.e., by overcoming both economic fear and prejudice. A second vicious circle is equally dangerous. The undereducated Negro cannot fill skilled jobs; yet such jobs have been denied Negroes so long that the Negro youth has little incentive to gain education. Again the circle must be broken on both sides.

5. Special efforts will be needed for some specific problems such as housing and health. Housing is costly, especially in urban areas. Even when people have the money to pay for it, there simply is not enough adequate housing for everybody. Visitors from other much poorer countries are often amazed that American cities permit their vast and miserable slums. The problems in health services are in some ways similar. Hospitalization is increasingly expensive, and some hospitals (especially for mental illness) are entirely inadequate to needs. American society, despite experiments in the areas of housing and health, has not yet decided how it will meet these needs.

[5] *New York Times,* Mar. 8, 1964, "News of the Week in Review."

6. When everything else is done, there will always remain (as in any society) some people who are not able to earn a living. Because of illness or disability, ignorance, stupidity, or personal maladjustment, they do not fit in. Every society provides some way to take care of them. A well-organized society can reduce the unemployables below the number America now has, but it cannot eliminate their problem. Call it relief, dole, or anything else, something must be offered to those who cannot earn a living. It can be generous enough to avoid cruelty without becoming so lavish that normally lazy people will prefer to stop working.

These six elements of a solution are all well known. To some extent American society has worked on them all. We must ask, therefore, why so wealthy a society has not accomplished more.

WHY POVERTY PERSISTS

Throughout most of human history poverty has been inevitable. Drudgery and hunger were part of life. Goods were scarce. Nations did not attempt to get rid of poverty because there was no use in trying.

Sometimes because of habit we still think in the old patterns. We quote—and misinterpret—a saying of Jesus: "You always have the poor with you" (Matt. 26:11). But the world has changed. Poverty is not a necessity but an evil, an injustice, an offense against mankind. It need not persist, but still it does.

One reason is that poverty is a complex reality that will take all our will and wits to conquer. We cannot put money in a slot, push a button, and pull out wealth for everyone. Any process that requires more jobs, better racial relations, improved public education, and the overcoming of defeatism in many families is an immense job.

A successful war against poverty must be fought in thousands of localities by police departments, public health services, school boards, sanitation departments, civic organizations, and churches. It must also be fought on a national scale. It will require new ideas from economists, sociologists, educators, and politicians. It will require new programs in government, industry, and labor movements. All in all it will require so much effort and skill that some think it cannot be done. But a society that can build supersonic aircraft and send rockets to the moon can solve the problem of poverty—when it wants to make the effort.

That brings us to a second reason for the delay. Americans have not yet convinced themselves that they should make the necessary effort. Part of the reason is complacency and greed. When the majority of people are prosperous, they forget about the rest.

Society helps by hiding poverty. Most of us rarely see the desperately poor. They live in city slums that we usually avoid or in rural slums that are invisible from the superhighways. They seldom vote. They do not show up in most churches or stores or parks. Many citizens simply cannot believe the documented facts reported in this chapter. When America sees the poor and when the poor make it impossible for all of us to forget them, we will decide to do something.

A third reason for inaction has to do with a typical American attitude. This society is devoted to free enterprise and is suspicious of big government. The conquest of poverty will require major action by government, local and federal. Government alone cannot do the job, but nobody can do it apart from government. However, there is no reason to think that it will mean delegating as much power to government as is done in wartime—or as much unaccountable power as America gives the Central Intelligence Agency in peacetime. Long ago the opponents of big government attacked social security; now Americans enjoy it and both political parties regularly vote to raise the benefits—usually just before elections. Some day we will expect similar governmental action to defeat poverty.

Such action will require expenditures of money, perhaps an unbalanced budget. Here we meet a typical example of the American suspicion of government: society takes one attitude toward governmental debt and quite a different attitude toward individual or corporate debt. The dislike of debt has a sound basis. To spend money extravagantly or to buy things without figuring how to pay for them is irresponsible. But in everything except government, we distinguish between different types of debt.

There are debts incurred because we are not paying the normal costs of living; these are dangerous. But there are debts that actually strengthen our financial position; these, if carefully handled, are desirable.

Most families recognize this difference. Suppose we compare two families. Family A pays rent for 15 years and never goes into debt. Family B buys a house with a mortgage loan. After 15 years the two families have these financial records:

	Assets	*Debts*
Family A	Car, $3,000 in savings	None
Family B	$25,000 house, car, $1,000 in savings	$5,000 mortgage on the house

Anybody would say that Family B is better off, despite its debt—probably because it went into debt. If the parents of Family B die, the children will not complain about inheriting a debt.

Corporations reason the same way. Almost any expanding corporation incurs debts. If it used only current income to finance expansion, it would never keep up with the times.

Applying the same reasoning to government, we should expect to avoid waste and extravagance, never postponing payments carelessly or self-indulgently. We should beware of expenditures that cause inflation. But we should expect the government to acquire debts that strengthen the country for the future. The next generation will be better off with a strong economy and reasonable debts than with a limping economy and no debts.

Now let us look at the record of American debt from 1946 to 1963. We find that corporation debts multiplied about four times. Individual and noncorporate debts multiplied about six times. State and local governmental debts increased still more. Federal debt increased far less than any of the others, considerably less than one-fourth.

If we compare the federal debt to the strength of the economy (as a family compares its debt to its income), we see something that is rarely pointed out: the debt dropped from 123 per cent of the Gross National Product in 1946 to about 55 per cent in 1963. Looking at the subject another way, in 1946 the federal debt was 57.8 per cent of the total debt (private and public) of the American people; by 1963 it was 23.9 per cent.[6]

All these data are not part of a slick game with numbers. This is an effort to see federal debt as we normally look at other debts. The debt has increased in actual dollars since World War II, but far less than other debts. In relation to the economic strength behind the debt, it has decreased. Yet the public worries far more about the federal share of the debt than about the rest.

Nothing here is meant to be a call for lax financial practices. However, if victory over poverty requires governmental money, we should consider the expenditures in the same rational way that we consider nongovernmental expenditures.

ACTION NOW

There are two reasons why America should do something about poverty now. The first reason comes out of plain, intelligent self-interest. The poor are not doing their share to strengthen the country, and they cannot so long as they remain extremely poor. They are not producing. They are not consuming enough to raise profits for the rest of us. They are not strengthening us in our international rivalries. They are a drag on the society. We would be smart to get them working, spending, learning, and improving themselves.

The second reason is a more generous one. We have an opportunity to help the poor, to relieve suffering, to open up hope for frustrated people. Moral sensitivity and human understanding demand that we do what we reasonably can.

Long ago the prophet Isaiah (3:15) wrote:

> "What do you mean by crushing my people,
> by grinding the face of the poor?"
> says the Lord God of hosts.

A few centuries later Jesus of Nazareth said that he had come "to preach good news to the poor" (Luke 4:18).

[6] See National Industrial Conference Board, *Road Maps of Industry*, No. 1486 (June 19, 1964). Also James W. Kuhn, *Christians Face Issues of High Moment in Our Changing Economy* (New York: National Council of Churches, 1962), p. 30.

What do these sayings mean to us today? Here is something for us to think about as we go to church, to work, and to the polls.

5 | The Organized Society

A BUSY STREET INTERSECTION at rush hour is a familiar symbol of modern society. Traffic lights control the movement of cars and people. Everybody would like to go at the same time—and as fast as possible. But if everybody did, the result would be chaos. There has to be a system that says some may move and others must wait. Those who wait know that their turn to move will come. They probably grow impatient with the system, but they know it is needed. In the long run the system benefits everybody.

Every driver is familiar with another experience. He reaches an intersection when no traffic is in sight. The law and his training cause him to stop and wait for the red light to change. He sees no logical reason to stop except that the system demands it. He favors the system. But at this moment it means that some administrators far away, who do not see this driver or know he is here, are forcing him to stop. Organization, although we need it, frustrates us.

Often organization helps us, often it irks us. Always we must learn to live with it.

THE DRIVE TOWARD ORGANIZATION

To some extent all societies are organized. A beehive or a flock of birds is an organization. Human beings always develop some kind of organization. Whether they live in primitive tribes or modern civilizations, they have their practices, customs, and institutions. These govern the relations between parents and children, men and women, those who give orders and those who take them.

American society is especially highly organized. When many people live close together in a high-speed, technological society, they need intricate organization. The desire for a high standard of living, for economic security, for military defense, for dependability in production and services, for political efficiency, for health and education—these are some of the impulses that push us toward increasing organization.

The familiar example of a morning breakfast tells something about the nature of the organized society. The coffee came from a plantation far away. It reached the breakfast table because of a corporation and its employees, a ship and a crew, some longshoremen, a wholesaler, a trucking firm, and a retailer. There are similar stories behind the sugar, the toast, and every item of food —plus the refrigerator that held the food and the stove that cooked it. The meal depends upon innumerable people in many far-flung organizations.

Europeans and Asians frequently smile at the love of organization in the United States. In Europe it is sometimes said that if four Americans parachute from a plane, by the time they reach the ground they will have a president, vice-president, secretary, and treasurer. But Europe and Asia are becoming more organized too. Modern organization is contagious because modern styles of life demand organization.

One evidence of the importance of organizations is the office. Only recently in human history have offices become so important a part of life. Today millions of people in technological societies work in offices. And those who rarely go near offices find their lives constantly related to offices. If the family has a credit card or a few charge accounts, its credit rating is on file in an office, and secretaries keep the family's records in several other offices. If the family has a bank account, another office is part of its life. If it has an insurance policy, that means another office. If the family pays income tax or has one or more social security numbers, it belongs to one of the biggest office systems of all.

Even the home is likely to be highly organized. Probably the family sets the alarm clock by figuring the time when the children must leave for school or the father start for work. Many a mother lives by a weekly schedule. Monday she drives the neighborhood children to school and picks them up. Tuesday she takes one of the children to the dentist, and Wednesday she goes to a committee of the P.T.A. Thursday she visits the supermarket and buys the groceries for the week ahead, and Friday she is den mother for the cub scouts. When mother's life is like that, obviously the children's lives are organized too.

For better and for worse modern life is organized. Modern man survives within organization. He makes a living by meeting the demands of organization. When he goes places, whether one mile or 100 miles away, organization offers him the possibilities and the limits of action. If he wants to fight the organization, he probably joins an organization for the purpose. To be an individual he depends upon organization.

HUMAN RELATIONS

It is easy to see what organizations accomplish in terms of production, research, and other objective achievements. It is harder to discover accurately what they are doing to the persons who live within them and depend upon them. But this latter is surely the important issue.

We sometimes hear that organization tends to make life impersonal. Like all sweeping statements, that one includes some truth and some error. We need to examine it.

In some ways modern life does get impersonal. To cite a personal example, I remember the time when the postman delivered a Christmas card signed with a name that no one in the family recognized. The man who sent it guessed that we would not recognize it, because under his name he wrote, "Your milkman." Day in and day out, he had been making life convenient for us, but we did not know his name and would not have recognized him if we had met him on the street. When I was a boy, I knew the milkman because he rang doorbells on Saturday and collected his bills. But now the bills come from an office and people pay by mail. Some of us never meet, never see, never learn the name of the milkman.

In factories men often scarcely know the workers quite close to them on the assembly line. In one extreme case two men worked in the same room, occasionally talked to each other, but never became well acquainted. One day one of them took the afternoon off, to go to his son's wedding. The other took the same afternoon off, to go to his daughter's wedding. The two were startled to meet each other at the same marriage ceremony. Middle-class people find that hard to believe, but it happened. It is an extravagant case, but things like that go on in the organized society.

A common feature of modern American society is the IBM card. One small card represents a person. Each little slot on the card tells something about the person. The perforations may indicate a man's age, his skills, his seniority, his pay, his status, his IQ, his credit rating, his emotional qualities—everything about him that matters for certain purposes.

Those cards can be a great help to persons. Because of them a man's business accounts, his insurance policies, his claims with the Veterans' Administration or the social security agency can be handled quickly and accurately. The card is a "stand-in" for the person. For some purposes it is far better to have the card in the right office than to go to the office oneself.

However, to speak personally, I do not want anybody to forget that *I* am not a card. I am stubborn enough to insist that I can do things that the card cannot do. And I am glad that—at least part of the time—my wife and children would rather have me around than the card.

The cards are having a major effect on the shape of our society. The people who make them know that. International Business Machines has given Harvard University $5 million to study the social effects of modern machines. Thomas J. Watson, Jr., chairman of the company, has said: "Hopefully this work will help to generate the understanding and ideas our country needs to get the full benefits of technology while minimizing disruptions and hardships." [1]

Often it is argued that modern organization brings advantages of efficiency at the cost of the warmer personal relations of

[1] *New York Times*, May 15, 1964.

past societies. When the case is put that way, the moral advantage seems to be with the past. But organization can bring moral gains. For example, most corporations have worked out generous plans for sick leave and health insurance for their employees. The cost of individual sickness is thus distributed throughout the organization. This is the organized method of bearing one another's burdens.

There are even some moral gains—along with the dangers so often announced—in the development of the "organization man." Certainly the "other-directed" person, who has so lost his purposes that he does not know what to do or even how to feel without taking his cues from society, is not a heroic character.[2] And the organization man may lose all personal integrity as he becomes a weak reflection of the system within which he works.[3] Insofar as organization changes creative, purposeful people into bland, inoffensive puppets, it devitalizes humanity.

But organization need not, and certainly does not always, enslave individuals and destroy their integrity. No doubt organization should make special efforts to appreciate determined individuals who chafe under the system and its demands for conformity. But organization by its nature impresses men with the interdependence of human life and the need that people have for each other. Cooperation, as truly as individualism, has moral value. It is not clear that the old-fashioned rugged individualist, who eyed every man as his competitor, had richer human relations than the modern man, who must work with many others in an organization.

FREEDOM AND ORGANIZATION

As organization replaces many of the older forms of individualism, it changes the nature of freedom. In an organized world, people have to work together. At some points in life everybody takes orders. Somebody or some sign is always telling us what to do.

[2] David Riesman, et al., The Lonely Crowd (Garden City, N.Y.: Doubleday Anchor Book, 1953).

[3] William H. Whyte, Jr., The Organization Man (Garden City, N.Y.: Doubleday Anchor Book, 1957; first published, 1956) .

The modern superhighway with its intricate interchanges is a case in point. On a simpler road system, when the driver wants to go left, he makes a left turn. On the modern interchange he does better to forget his sense of direction, ignore his mental picture of the area, and simply obey orders. Somebody else has figured out the best way. The driver watches the maze of signs and obeys them.

There are days when life seems to be mostly a series of signs: STOP . . . GO . . . NO LEFT TURN . . . NO U-TURN . . . NO TURNS . . . NO SPITTING . . . CURB YOUR DOG . . . WALK, DON'T RUN . . . KEEP MOVING—DON'T LOITER . . . NO SMOKING . . . NO BALL PLAYING . . . DON'T PICK FLOWERS . . . DON'T TALK TO DRIVER . . . HAVE EXACT CHANGE . . . DON'T FEED THE ANIMALS . . . CROSS ON THE GREEN, NOT IN BETWEEN . . . KEEP OFF THE GRASS . . . PARKING STRICTLY FORBIDDEN . . . DON'T BE A LITTERBUG . . . KEEP RIGHT . . . SQUEEZE LEFT . . . SLOW DOWN . . . MAINTAIN SPEED ON INCLINE . . . PUT COIN IN TURNSTILE . . . MOVE TO THE BACK OF THE BUS . . . LET THEM OUT . . . PAY TAXES HERE . . . SIGN ON THE DOTTED LINE.

All this has a purpose, but it can be frustrating. I recall my experience as an army recruit when a sergeant explained the system of authority. "Privates," he said, "take orders from officers and noncommissioned officers. The officers and N.C.O.'s take orders from higher officers, and they take orders from the commanding general of the division. He takes orders from the corps commander and from the big brass in Washington. And everybody in the army takes orders from the Commander-in-Chief, the President." Then the sergeant turned on a triumphant grin and continued: "And who do you suppose the Commander-in-Chief takes orders from? Why, from you, the voters!"

It sounded fine, but it gave us little satisfaction when the sergeant ordered us to do something we did not like. Sometimes the organized society seems increasingly like that. We take more and more orders, and we derive less and less satisfaction from giving orders—or, more important, from deciding things for ourselves.

Some help comes in distinguishing two kinds of freedom: freedom *from*—that is, freedom from external controls and from orders; and freedom *to*—freedom to accomplish what we want to do. If we think mainly of freedom *from*, the organized society has cut down our freedom. For anybody who thinks freedom means that nobody will tell him what to do, freedom is vanishing. But if we think mainly of freedom *to*, we find many gains. Organization often increases the possibilities and the choices before us. A person today has freedoms his grandparents never knew: freedom to cross the country in a few hours, to get jobs that did not exist a generation ago, to read from a tremendous variety of inexpensive books.

Peter F. Drucker, the famous economist, has put the issue in terms of an example:

> Less than a generation ago, all a mathematician, for instance, could do, as a rule, was to teach. Today there is no counting the directions in which he can go, the jobs in which he can apply mathematics, the organizations and institutions in which he can find a livelihood, a career and social effectiveness.
>
> But at the same time, these, increasingly, are opportunities *within* the large organizations. Fewer and fewer can make a living or become effective outside.[4]

Thus organization changes the nature of freedom. It cuts down some freedoms, enhances others. And its effect is as great on the inner as on the outer dimensions of freedom. That is, the organized society not only sets the possibilities for acting freely. It also, as we have seen, influences our hidden desires as we try to relate personal integrity to the pressures of the system for conformity. In the years ahead we can expect many experiments, both enticing and painful, as mankind seeks to realize freedom in an increasingly organized world.

THE HUMAN IMPORTANCE OF STRUCTURES

As we learn to live in this new, highly organized society, we have to make decisions that never confronted our forefathers. To make them responsibly we must learn to recognize the human importance and the moral importance of organizations and in-

[4] Peter F. Drucker, "Our Emerging Industrial Society," an address delivered at the Fourth National Study Conference on the Church and Economic Life, sponsored by the National Council of Churches, Pittsburgh, Penn., Nov. 8, 1962.

stitutions. We cannot be content to think of morality solely in terms of personal integrity, generosity, and compassion. Increasingly we must look at the moral meaning of institutional structures and processes.

Our world is full of examples. Some of the striking ones come from international affairs. Sometimes the American people, moved by a combination of self-interest and good will, have tried to help another country suffering from poverty. Churches and other voluntary agencies have sent people and money. Congress, with its usual reluctance, has voted economic aid. The Peace Corps has given educational and engineering help. Everybody regarded these as ethical acts. But while all this was going on, a change of one cent a pound in the prices of coffee and cocoa did more harm to the economy than all the efforts to help it. Nobody regarded the price change as an ethical issue; in fact it represented no decision at all. It resulted from many unpredictable events—the size of crops, changes in shipping costs, maybe a labor controversy or two, a shift of housewives' preferences from regular to instant coffee. These miscellaneous forces, which have no ethical purpose, so changed vast organizational processes as to wipe out a deliberate moral effort of people and governments.

To report such events does not take us far toward deciding what we should do. The right decisions depend upon skills that we have not yet developed adequately—partly because we have barely begun to see their importance. But one thing is immediately clear: We shall not progress far in offering better opportunities to people unless we examine the structures and workings of the vast organizations in which they—and we—live.

In every discussion of a social problem somebody sooner or later says: "The way to get a better world is to get better people," or, "The answer to that social problem [war, racial tensions, disputes between capital and labor] is to change the hearts of men." By this time in history that judgment has surely been proved wrong. We always need better people and changed hearts. But we also need better institutions to implement human generosity, to thwart human evil, and to channel organizational processes that unintentionally hurt as well as help people.

In an age when a slight change in interest rates can touch off either inflation (which hurts people on fixed incomes, especially aged people) or deflation (which means that people lose jobs), it is not enough to say that the Federal Reserve Board should be made up of good men. Of course those men should be good—incorruptible, committed to human welfare, beyond suspicion of selfish motivation in their duties. But they should also understand the workings of a complex fiscal and economic system. That system with all its processes can do more to help and hurt people than the good and evil acts of many persons within it.

At exactly this point our civilization requires some fresh thinking. Ethical traditions, coming out of earlier times, do not inform us about modern organizations. The great German scholar, Ernst Troeltsch, described one problem of the modern Christian in his book, *The Social Teachings of the Christian Churches*:

> Christianity has a distinct leaning towards comparatively simple conditions of living. . . . It also has a leaning towards little groups and corporations which are closely bound together in personal relationships, in which the formal legal and economic tendency of a dehumanized and abstract organization of the common life has not yet forced personal relationships and decisions into the sphere of isolated instances.[5]

This does not mean that the Christian today has ethical insight superior to the New Testament's. The Christian believes that the New Testament brings him an understanding of God and man that is basic to all his human relations and decisions. He must discover the meaning and implications of the biblical faith and understanding for modern situations that are not mentioned in the Bible. And this is a big undertaking.

All the major traditional religions and ethical philosophies have comparable gaps that their contemporary disciples must fill. These teachings were not developed in our kind of world. Without forgetting them or betraying them, contemporary man has to discover their meaning for today.

I suggested, in Chapter 1, that we do not get complete guidance for today merely by repeating old commandments, even the

[5] Ernst Troeltsch, *The Social Teachings of the Christian Churches*, trans. by Olive Wyon (New York: Macmillan, 1931), Vol. 1, p. 86.

profound biblical command, "You shall love your neighbor as
yourself" (Matt. 22:39). Let us return to that point in the setting of the organized society. Certainly we cannot think up a
better ethical principle to replace the old one. But we have a
major job in discovering the actual meaning for today of love for
"the neighbor."

The same is true of the Golden Rule. Repeatedly people say,
"We'd solve all our problems if everybody would just follow the
Golden Rule." But that talk does not get us very far. Of course
the world would be better if more people lived by the Golden
Rule: "Do unto others as you would have them do unto you." I
am glad that most of the world's great religions have a Golden
Rule or something close to it. But the Golden Rule is only a
starting point, not a conclusion, for the issues of the organized
society.

Think of the many decisions that must be made in the modern economy. The Golden Rule and love of neighbor can find
expression in those decisions. But no traditional rule or command will itself prescribe the complex relations between management, stockholders, and laborers. No ethical rule tells management how to make a better product or how to meet competition
and still be generous to employees. No command tells the retailer
how to keep up with competitors, please a capricious public,
advertise legitimately, and serve the real needs of the community
while remaining solvent.

Think too of the life of a family in a city or a suburban
development. Perhaps the family truly believes in the traditional
commandments and seeks to live by them. The troubled father
must still discover how to divide his time between his job and his
family. The parents must think as citizens about the tax rate and
how the public budget should be divided among schools, roads,
sanitation, and police protection. All members of the family
must learn how to live on congenial terms with their neighbors
and yet preserve their own character and individuality.

When Jesus explained the meaning of love for the neighbor,
he told the story of the Good Samaritan. There love of neighbor
expressed itself in direct, personal helpfulness to a man in need.
That kind of good deed, in a face-to-face relation, will always be

important. Human society will never outgrow it. But the organized society demands more. It requires that we develop institutions that will help the neighbor whom we do not meet face to face.

Once men did enough when they helped the needy persons whom they met. The next step was to establish organizations—church agencies, United Givers Funds, the Red Cross—in order to help neighbors beyond immediate sight. The further step is to organize society so that few neighbors will need charity, so that more can support their families and live in their old age without asking for mercy from the more prosperous. Then, when organization has done all that it can, we shall still need to cultivate direct personal relations between men and their neighbors.

POWER AND RESPONSIBILITY

One further issue confronts organized society. This society characteristically requires great concentrations of power. In a huge, interrelated society concentrated power is necessary if anything is to get done. But concentrated power can be risky.

I once had the opportunity to discuss this issue among a group of men and women chosen from positions of leadership in industry, business, labor, agriculture, government, education, and the church. All quickly agreed that our society concentrates power to a dangerous degree in some organizations, but there was no agreement at all on which these organizations were. The industrialist felt powerless in the face of big labor and big government, while labor and agriculture were sure that industry had overwhelming power. Each group was sure that its power was not too great, but that somebody else's threatened the society.

Without settling all the arguments, we can immediately see that many organizations in our society possess great power. But then we meet a paradox. The ability to use this concentrated power is often spread among many men and groups, so that we have difficulty in locating it and fixing responsibility.

An American corporation, for example, may have a bigger annual income than the government of a major European nation. (Sales by General Motors Corporation in one year have surpassed the budget of France.) Traditionally the owners of wealth and power have been responsible for its use. But the owners of a corporation are its stockholders, and many corporations today have more stockholders than employees. (American Telephone and Telegraph Company has well over two million stockholders.) Some stockholders are investors in mutual funds, who do not even know what their holdings are. It is plain enough that these stockholders are not exercising much responsibility for the use of the corporation's power. It is management that wields the power.

But who sees to it that management uses its power for good? The stockholders might, except that they are too numerous and too ignorant of the inner workings of the company. Labor unions do at a few points, but not at many. Government, through courts and regulatory agencies, exercises some supervision. And management itself through its own moral qualities may show responsibility. But the whole set-up is complex. Occasionally, when law has been violated, it appears that nobody in the entire corporation will take responsibility for the illegal acts.

The same issue arises in labor unions. Theoretically the members control the organization, but by the time a strike vote is taken, the result is usually a foregone conclusion. And the members seldom have any way of knowing if one of their officials has practiced misconduct, unless the courts find him guilty.

Government is comparable. According to the democratic ideal the people are basically responsible for their government. But the average citizen has little to do with deciding policy in Southeast Asia or even in Washington. The power of the United States government is tremendous; it is not always easy to know who wields that power.

The organized society still has to learn more about the best ways of concentrating power and holding it responsible. This challenge exists, not only on the big scale, but in small organizations as well. The organized society is not something distant, but is part of everybody's life in a country like the United States. Each citizen—in schools, businesses, labor organizations, civic clubs, government, churches—can learn what these organizations are doing to himself and to other people.

There is no point in complaining about the organized society. Today most things are done through organizations. But
human beings are in the organizations. They can insist that organizations are meant to serve men, not men to serve organizations.

6 | Metropolitan Society

ONE OF THE GREAT NEW FACTS in modern civilization is the emer-
gence of metropolitan society. This means at least three things:
(1) People are moving by the millions from the country to the
city—or are sitting still while the city expands into the country
to include them. (2) Metropolitan areas bind together many
cities and towns with a common transportation network and common economic processes. (3) The shrinking minority who live
in the country come to think and act increasingly like city
people.

The America that many people cherish, especially at
Christmas time, is the America of Currier and Ives or maybe of
Grandma Moses. But the America in which we live is vastly
different. Colonial America was rural. But by 1900 the nation
was 40 per cent urban. And by 1960 it was 70 per cent urban.
Furthermore, only 9 per cent of the people live on farms, where
most people once lived. Within this century American society has
changed from dominantly rural to dominantly urban.

Urbanization is going on throughout most of the world. The
rate is faster in Japan, the Soviet Union, and Puerto Rico than it
has ever been in continental America. In Africa the number of
people living in cities of 100,000 population increased over the

first 50 years of this century by 629 per cent.[1] Because of the combination of the population explosion and urbanization, the world will need as many new homes in the next 40 years as it has built in the whole of human history up to now.[2]

Urbanization is not a smooth, steady process. It consists of many chaotic migrations. Newcomers from the country and from overseas move into the hearts of the cities, while the older residents as they become prosperous move outward to suburbs. The American Negroes are perhaps the most swiftly urbanized, easily identifiable group in all history. They have changed from an overwhelmingly rural people to dwellers in the most tightly packed urban ghettos in the land. The change brings excitement and pathos, opportunity and tragedy. Society has barely begun to understand and to deal with the dynamic, confusing, revolutionary process of urbanization.

THE LURE AND THE AGONY OF THE CITY

The city prompts strong feelings. To some the word "city" is a reminder of citizen, of civilization. To others it is one of the four-letter words, standing for a parasitic growth that mars the countryside. Mention Athens and people think of the glory that was Greece, the triumphs of human art, intellect, and imagination. Mention Babylon and many think of the beast and the whore. The difference rests only in part on empirical evidence of two ancient cities. Every city is both magnet and monster. Thus ancient Rome represented the forum, the Senate, the tribunes of the people, the Roman law. And ancient Rome was, in the language of Tacitus, the sewer into which flowed "all things horrible and disgraceful."

The most intensely urbanized concentration in the United States is on an island named after the Manhattan Indians. People are stacked in there at a density of 77,195 per square mile. It happens to be the urban area that I know best, love and worry

---

[1] The data come from the research staff of the United Nations Bureau of Social Affairs. See Julia J. Henderson, "Urbanization and the World Community," *Annals of the American Academy of Political and Social Science*, Vol. 314 (Nov., 1957), pp. 147, 148.

[2] Barbara Ward, reviewing Charles Abrams, *Man's Struggle for Shelter in an Urbanizing World*, the *New York Times Book Review*, Aug. 10, 1964.

over the most. The Frenchman, Jean-Paul Sartre, has called it a "desert of rock." It has been cursed for its slums, its crime, its politics, its greed. But E. B. White writes that Manhattan "is like poetry: it compresses all life, all races and breeds, into a small island and adds music and the accompaniment of internal engines." It is "the greatest human concentrate on earth, the poem whose magic is comprehensible to millions of permanent residents but whose full meaning will always remain illusive." [3]

Go to Chicago, Cleveland, Detroit, St. Louis, Los Angeles, San Francisco, Dallas, New Orleans, Washington, Philadelphia —and you will find similar differences of opinion. Go to the smaller cities, to the towns of 10,000 people (increasingly being swept into metropolitan orbits)—in any city you will find the alluring and the repelling.

The words connected with the city all have a double emotional impact. "Urban" may mean urbane, humane, cultured; it may mean urban sprawl, ugly destruction of values in the chase for profit, the frustration of persons by mechanisms. "Metropolis" may evoke thoughts of slums, of rats, of delinquency; or it may stir the exhilaration of professional opportunities and enjoyment of the arts. People discover in the city partly what they fear to meet, partly what they want to meet, partly what the city invites them to meet.

Whether we like it or not, the city is part of modern America and the modern world. Whether we live in it or not, we must learn to live with it. Even rural man, if he has a car, a telephone, and a television set, has become urbanized. So today inner city, suburbs, and countryside must all come to terms with metropolis.

RECOGNIZING THE CITY

Since the city is inside us as well as outside us, it is not as easy to recognize as we might suppose. It may help to think of the city as three things. It is at least all of these, and no one of them tells the whole story.[4]

[3] E. B. White, *Here Is New York* (New York: Harper & Row, 1949), pp. 21-22.

[4] For two profound and original analyses of the city see Max Weber, *The City* (New York: Collier Books, 1962) and Lewis Wirth, "Urbanism as a Way of Life," *American Journal of Sociology*, Vol. 44 (July, 1938), pp. 1-24.

First, the city is a fact of geography. It is visible and tangible —the city that nobody can fail to recognize. No one flying over a city mistakes it for a ranch or a forest. It is buildings—homes, factories, warehouses, offices, stores, schools, churches—crowded together and often heaped high into the air. It is streets, vehicles, and people massed close together.

This is the city that demographers, architects, cartographers, and sociologists can survey and measure. They can locate inner city and suburbs, residential and industrial areas, main channels of traffic, mansions and slums, ghettos and areas of wide human interaction. Any square mile of city includes a fantastic network of buildings, streets, wires, pipes, and mechanisms. The whole array has qualities of permanence but it is always changing. It is by any account an impressive pile of stuff. Anybody moving around in it keeps meeting this stuff as obstacles and as things to be used.

Second, the city is a set of social relationships and organized institutions. These are not so tangible as the people and structures, but they operate in many evident ways. The relationships include the patterns of industry, commerce, law and government, education, religion, recreation. They are modes of operation for competitive and cooperative activities. Their structure is determined partly by paper (laws, charters, constitutions, rules of procedure), partly by custom and habit, partly by the purposes of people, partly by the physical layout of the city (i.e., the city in the first meaning).

A city in this second sense is a set of ways for getting things done. It is an organized life that makes possible intercourse between buyer and seller, contractor and subcontractor, professional and client. The yellow pages of the telephone directory offer clues to this jumble of relationships. Everybody is familiar with some of them, and nobody knows them all.

Third, the city is a mentality. It is a complex of ideas, attitudes, qualities of living and feeling. It is a mingling of confusion and clarity, of pride and frustration. It is a pace of life, a way of responding to situations, a spirit that penetrates into people and shapes their characters.

The city in this third sense is less visible and tangible than in the first two senses, but it is no mystic dream. It is a powerful agent, obviously different from the cave, the farm, or the sea. It has been observed that a country man can become a city man, but that the city man does not readily become a country man. He may move to a country estate to get away from it all; but wherever he goes, he takes the city with him.

The city as we know it is all three of these things. And this composite of people and objects, of functions and relations, of ideas and attitudes has further characteristics. A few, which have major significance for human living and decisions, are worth noting.

1. A traditional function of the city is mutual support and protection of persons. In past history this function has often meant fortifications and common defense against attackers. That function is gone. In a world where everything is vulnerable, the city is most vulnerable of all. Today the hospital, the fire apparatus, and the safety department are better symbols than walls and cannon for the function of mutual support.

2. The city is the place where men make their living in commerce, industry, the professions, and services rather than in agriculture. Furthermore the city encourages refined division of labor and specialization of function, as well as the availability of many goods. City man and country man—each develops personality qualities, peculiar kinds of shrewdness and naïveté, that go with his economy. These characteristics have been the subject of comedy through the centuries.

3. The city is a market place, not only of commodities, but also of culture. It attracts scholars, scientists, writers, actors, painters. Rural life produces its regional arts, which deserve appreciation in a day of mass culture; but for every Grandma Moses there are 100 young artists who seek the city. Today, to be sure, radio, cinema, television, and paperback books reach everywhere; but they move out from the city. Among its many people every kind of creativity and idiosyncrasy can flourish. The dominant cultural centers are inevitably urban.

4. The city apparently requires a large role of government. For instance, in the country drinking-water comes from wells, but not in the city. Many square miles of country need no govern-

ment property or construction; every square mile of city is honey-combed with streets and sewers, and crisscrossed daily with buses and service vehicles owned or regulated by government. The city readily becomes the center of the political machine. And despite the increase of government and police power, it is an arena for crime.

5. Urban life provides a large role for abstract forms and processes. Wealth is a good example. Originally wealth meant land and tangible objects. In urban society money became impor-tant. At first money was of metal, a concrete embodiment of wealth. Then it came to be of paper, a more abstract symbol of wealth, which is remotely and fractionally related to silver or gold, but represents in large part an intricate credit structure. Even more abstract are stocks and bonds, representing a corpo-rate structure, the competence of management, good will, and guesses about the future. Another urban abstraction is time. In the metropolis time is largely separated from the pulse of nature, the rhythms of fatigue and refreshment. It is the abstract time of clocks, the time that sets and limits appointments, time cali-brated to a scale that adjusts the natural seasonal hours to the needs of human institutions. I do not object to these abstractions. Abstract thinking is a human triumph; but, as Alfred North Whitehead insisted, we should remember that it is abstract.

As society becomes increasingly urbanized, these various characteristics of the city tend to become qualities of our whole society. They present modern man with issues that call for thought and decisions.

MAN AND NATURE

One of these issues is the relation between man and nature. Man, whatever else he may be, is part of nature—born of it, akin to it. Does urban man, hiding or even defying this kinship, cut away at his own roots and enervate his life? In the city, as else-where, we are aware of nature. We notice the seasons, the weather. Occasionally we may see a sunset or even look at the stars overhead. But increasingly the man-made environment is more noticeable than the natural environment.

Arnold Toynbee, reflecting upon the future of religion, said that one of man's great traditional religions is gone, never to return: the worship of nature as the Magna Mater, the great Earth-Mother. We have learned to use nature rather than to adore her, and we cannot worship our servant.[5] Perhaps we should not regret the loss. Judaism and Christianity have always regarded nature-worship as a heresy. But we may still ask what risks lie in a total irreverence for nature. Ancient man said: "I lift up my eyes to the hills" (Ps. 121:1)—and he thought of God. If man lifts up his eyes to the hills only to calculate their mineral resources for the sake of plunder, has he perhaps killed something within himself?

There is a false religion that likes to keep man feeble and dependent in order to keep him pious. We need none of that. But it is interesting to find in Dietrich Bonhoeffer, that thoroughly modern theologian who exults in man's strength and his ability to do without the support of conventional "religion," some signs of worry about urbanism. From the concentration camp where the Nazis were soon to kill him, he wrote to a nephew: "It would be much the best thing if you were brought up in the country." Realizing with some regret that the countryside was becoming urbanized, he wrote:

> Much as he needs solitude and peace, a man will find them very difficult to come by. But it will be an advantage amid all these changes to have beneath one's feet a few inches of soil from which to draw the resources for a new, natural, unpretentious and contented day's work and evening's leisure.[6]

Similarly Albert Camus, that magnificent French humanist and Nobel laureate in literature, worried about man's detachment from nature:

> We turn our backs on nature; we are ashamed of beauty. Our wretched tragedies have a smell of the office clinging to them and the blood that trickles from them is the colour of printer's ink. . . . We are thus living in the period of big cities. Deliberately, the

[5] Arnold Toynbee, *An Historian's Approach to Religion* (New York: Oxford University Press, 1956), pp. 230-231.

[6] Dietrich Bonhoeffer, *Prisoner for God* (New York: Macmillan, 1954), pp. 136-137.

world has been amputated of all that constitutes its permanence: nature, the sea, hilltops, evening meditation.[7]

Speaking personally, I happen to like the city better than Bonhoeffer and Camus did. But when I see bulldozers scooping up earth and tearing down trees, I wonder if they were not right. When I see people who rarely enjoy nature but think only how they can use it for profit, I have to agree that Bonhoeffer and Camus saw a truth.

Further it is worth noting that our time has had its difficulties in producing an urban poetry. Carl Sandburg, of course, wrote his poems of steel and exulted in Chicago, "hog butcher of the world." But we remember that Sandburg went on to collect folk songs from America's countryside, then to raise goats in Carolina. Perhaps from the insurance offices (where Wallace Stevens pursued one of his professions) or from the coffeehouses of Greenwich Village and San Francisco will come a genuinely urban poetry. So far I do not detect much joy in this poetry. And I wonder whether it is misplaced nostalgia or authentic appreciation that has led urban America to take to its heart only one recent poet, the adopted Vermonter, Robert Frost.

There is room for thought also in America's recreational habits. Once Saturday night was the time when the country came to town; now Friday afternoon to Sunday night is the time when as many city-dwellers as can move to the country. Fishing is America's favorite recreation. Most of the 35 million fishermen (and women) in this country are not Tom Sawyers wetting a line somewhere near home, but people who have made the effort to get from office and factory to lake and stream. The people who buy boats by the thousands seem unsure whether they want to go rural or want to urbanize the country with gas fumes, cocktail parties, and transistor radios; but they have some kind of yen for nature.

Curiously the people who are most ecstatic about the metropolis are usually those who can escape it. I have quoted from E. B. White's lyrical tribute to Manhattan. Since I like White's words, I hope I am not refuting them when I refer to the jacket

[7] Albert Camus, "Helen's Exile," in *The Myth of Sisyphus and Other Essays*, trans. by *Justin O'Brien* (London: Hamish Hamilton, 1955), p. 148.

of his book: "E. B. White . . . divides his time between New York City and a farm in Maine."

There is no point in romanticizing the country and forgetting the thrill of the city. One of the great human gifts is the ability to transform nature, to civilize life. But there is evidence that it is not good for man to sever his kinship with nature. In this urbanized world it becomes important to let ordinary people (not just the affluent) discover the kinship between man and nature. It is important that children know that milk comes from cows, and eggs from chickens, important to let them see plants and animals other than the tamed kinds that flourish in mass housing projects. It is important for man to build his cities and his civilization in nature without crushing nature.

There is a helpful pattern for our understanding in biblical faith, which is concerned more for history than for nature, yet never leaves nature behind. The great Jewish holidays celebrate history rather than nature. But often, scholars tell us, we have evidence of an initial nature-festival, transformed into a historical celebration that quite transcends but never obliterates its original meaning. Civilized man is historical man, a long way from natural man in any simple sense. But history builds upon, cultivates, disciplines, sublimates, and transmutes nature.

MAN AND MAN

As a second issue let us consider the relation between man and man in the urbanized world. We have already given attention to human relations in the organized society (Chapter 5). The metropolis is one great organization or complex of organizations, and it presents some special characteristics.

We shall be wise to start by discarding the foolish talk about the hardhearted city. Hardheartedness started in the Garden of Eden, and it has always been with man. Likewise we shall be wise to question the easy slogans about mass society and the depersonalizing of man in an urban world. But we should look at the facts that lead to the slogans.

One scholar has made this noteworthy observation:

The populations of many of our single metropolitan areas today are larger and more diverse than the whole United States at the time of its independence—all 13 colonies—so that the problems and potentialities of a metropolitan area are tremendously sophisticated and complex.[8]

When such is the case, it becomes humanly impossible for anyone to take a lively personal interest in more than a small fraction of the people in his metropolis. He can wish them all well, but he cannot know them all personally. The metropolis heightens our dependence upon others, but in a curiously impersonal way. The tendency to abstraction, which we have already noted in urban life, affects and afflicts human relations. We meet and treat each other as functions and roles, not as persons. How can one love his neighbor as himself when he has more neighbors than any one person can possibly meet? Love of neighbor has never been easy, because some neighbors are unlovely; but urbanization adds the difficulty of sheer numbers of neighbors.

Even more serious, urban life forces us to exclude deliberately from our awareness the needs of others. There are more needs than anyone can personally help to meet. For example, sitting in a downtown metropolitan office one day, I repeatedly heard the sirens of passing vehicles of the fire department. By the end of one day I had built up a habit of pushing those noises out of my consciousness. I had to if I was to get anything done. Then I recalled a midwestern village where, at every rare sound of the fire alarm, men dropped work or play to rush to their duties in the volunteer fire department. I puzzled about the contrast: they responded to the sound of need, while I hardened myself against the same sound. My act, I am sure, was rational. My taxes were supporting the fire department, which would do a better job if I stayed out of the way. The world would be no better off if I were to pause for a moment of concern every time the siren wailed.

Yet there is a danger in this deadening of sensitivity. Sometimes it has results that make us shudder. People train themselves to avoid "getting involved" in the troubles of others. Occasionally we read of some lurid crime that succeeded simply be-

[8] Dr. Edward Higbee, Professor of Geography and Land Utilization, University of Rhode Island, interviewed in *U. S. News and World Report* (June 22, 1964), p. 47.

cause people were unwilling to pay attention to the need of a neighbor.

However there is another side to the story. The urban life that can make us indifferent to others also opens the possibility for rich friendships. In traditional rural society a person knows the people who live in the neighborhood, and maybe a few relatives at a distance. In urban society he can seek out friends among a wide range of possibilities. He can join a group of Alcoholics Anonymous or of men who offer friendship to boys in adolescent gangs. He can gather with left-handed golfers, with friends who like exotic foods, with physicists and theologians who meet to educate each other. Urban man can enter a club of men who read *Moby Dick* once a year and meet to talk about it. Tall urbanites can join a club in which all the women are at least 5 feet, 10 inches tall and all the men are still taller. (I'm not inventing these examples; people have actually organized them.) The city offers comradeship for people of every conceivable concern. Friendships are not limited to the few available people in a small neighborhood; persons have unlimited opportunity to meet and enjoy others.

In another way the city enriches human relations. It is no accident that racial desegregation comes faster in urban than in rural areas. The metropolis throws together all breeds and classes of men. A minimal tolerance is the price of survival. An enlarged sympathy and understanding is the opportunity for imaginative people.

In these various ways, then, urbanization threatens and enhances human relations. Since human relations are the heart of any society, the metropolis dare not forget the personal needs of the people within it. Life is, above all else, personal. This elemental insight is an urgent need in the city. It is one reason why "urban renewal," seemingly an unquestionably good enterprise, is in fact so controversial. Critics like Lewis Mumford and Jane Jacobs, in widely differing ways, have blasted the planners who are more concerned for sanitation and symmetry than for people. The metropolis is buildings and streets, communications and utilities. But, more important, it is people.

DECISIONS AHEAD

By 1985, say some experts, two-thirds of the people of the United States will live on 10 per cent of the land. Four vast metropolitan areas are shaping up. The first and most crowded runs along the Eastern Seaboard from somewhere north of Boston to somewhere south of Washington. The second edges the Great Lakes from Buffalo to Chicago, then extends northward to Minneapolis–St. Paul and southward to St. Louis. The third is the rapidly growing West Coast. The fourth borders the Gulf of Mexico from Texas to Florida.

Are these changes an opportunity or a disaster? Will civilization respect nature or destroy it? Will we kill our human sensitivity as we get lost in the crowd, or will we learn to live in mutual appreciation?

The answers will be worked out in many ways. Let me suggest three.

First, we have to devise new methods of government. The old units and methods of government do not fit the new realities. For example, the metropolitan area surrounding New York City includes 1,467 governments.[9] Hardly any of the metropolitan problems can be solved by one government alone. Often the governments do not want to cooperate; they seem to exist for the sake of competition—that is, protecting one group of people against others or preserving the prestige of governmental officials. It is a wonder anything ever gets done about public education, crime, air and water pollution, traffic regulation and transit, fair taxation. The metropolis requires units of government big enough to grapple with its problems; yet it requires small units in order that people may participate in community affairs. Somehow this society must invent forms of government for today, not for the past.

Second, the churches have to make some decisions—above all the Protestant churches, whose traditional strongholds have been town and country. Will Herberg has summed up the Protestant record in a sentence:

[9] Robert C. Wood, *1400 Governments* (Cambridge, Mass.: Harvard University Press, 1961).

The story of American Protestantism is the story of a religious movement following the advancing frontier and subduing it, periodically crystallizing into established denominations, yet always in some way breaking through them again, until it comes face to face with what has so far proved an unsurmountable challenge, the urbanized, industrialized America of today.[10]

The easy answer is to move from the heart of the city and to put up new buildings in prosperous suburbs. There churches can enjoy comfortable surroundings and balance their budgets easily, while neglecting the downtown areas where men exercise power and people suffer in slums. They can quote poet T. S. Eliot:

O miserable cities of designing men.[11]

Or they can recognize "The City—God's Gift to the Church." [12] They can adapt their ministry to the whole city—power centers, slums, and suburbs—uniting their people in a concern for the common need.

Third, individuals face decisions. The ablest and luckiest can apply their wits to acquiring wealth, then move to luxury apartments or pleasant suburbs in order to escape the problems of the city. They can maneuver to escape taxation and the burdens of responsibility. Or they can, wherever they live, recognize that in this urban society they owe an obligation to the city. They can put the celebrated American ingenuity to creating more humane ways of life for all the people.

In her witty and perceptive book on modern cities Jane Jacobs has suggested that the present-day metropolis may soon answer the age-old question of man concerning the aim of life. The answer that she fears is: "The purpose of life is to produce and consume automobiles." [13] Those of us who want a better answer need to concern ourselves with the urbanization of life that is so speedily transforming America and the world. In the

[10] Will Herberg, *Protestant-Catholic-Jew* (Garden City, N.Y.: Doubleday, 1955), p. 113.

[11] Chorus from "The Rock," III.

[12] The title of a booklet issued by the Division of Evangelism and Department of the Urban Church, Board of National Missions, United Presbyterian Church in the U.S.A.

[13] Jane Jacobs, *The Death and Life of Great American Cities* (New York: Vintage Books, 1963; first published, 1961), p. 370.

metropolis, where increasingly men live, we can concentrate our energies on the changing relations that our civilization is bringing between man and his wealth, man and nature, man and his fellow man. If we do not act with urgency, fate will determine the course of our society before we have awakened.

7 | Racial Conflict and Reconciliation

THE GREATEST INTERNAL PROBLEM facing the United States of America is the racial problem. Similar conflicts exist in many parts of the world. In a few places, especially South Africa, the outlook is darker than in America. But nowhere are racial relations so momentous an issue for world history as in the United States. Most of the earlier chapters of this book have had to mention questions of race. Now we must face those questions head-on.

Mankind has often been torn apart by racial and ethnic quarrels. In Western history and perhaps even in the United States anti-Semitism has been the most vicious and the most persistent form of prejudice, a prejudice for which the Christian church bears much of the guilt. But the current worldwide revolution, which has come to a head in the city streets of America, is the revolution of the colored majority of mankind. They are seeking freedom, equality, a right to participate in the economic and cultural life of society. They are demanding that the white man make good on the slogans he has glibly pronounced for generations.

THE BITTER LEGACY AND "THE AMERICAN CREED"

The American people treasure their historic Declaration of Independence. But even the men who signed that document were not sure what they meant when they told the world that all men are created equal and are endowed by their Creator with inalienable rights. The original Constitution of the United States hedged shamefully on the issue of slavery.[1] Citizens have long repeated the pledge of allegiance to the flag, sometimes wondering about the last six words, "with liberty and justice for all."

On New Year's day, 1863, President Abraham Lincoln issued the Emancipation Proclamation, freeing all slaves in areas seceding from the Union. He did it as an act of war, limited in scope; but his words show that he believed it to be far more than that:

> And upon this act, sincerely believed to be an act of justice, warranted by the Constitution upon military necessity, I invoke the considerate judgment of mankind and the gracious favor of Almighty God.

The Thirteenth Amendment to the Constitution universalized emancipation throughout the United States.

More than a century after Lincoln's proclamation slavery, in the old sense of the word, is gone. But its wounds remain. In the industrial centers and the rural backlands of the South, dark-skinned men have been beaten and murdered because they sought to vote, to enter their children in public schools, to eat a sandwich at a lunch counter. In the metropolitan centers of the North, where these rights are guaranteed by law, colored people have risen in anger against an oppression that denies them employment and crowds them into ghettos of despair. "Negroes in this country," writes James Baldwin, "are taught really to despise themselves from the moment their eyes open on the world." [2]

Thus America still confronts the task of building a society where men may live together in freedom and mutual understanding. In "the land of the free and the home of the brave," some dark-skinned citizens have found that they have to be brave in

---

[1] Art. 1, sec. 2, without mentioning the word "slavery" provided that slaves, though they could not vote, would be counted at the rate of 60 per cent for purposes of representation in Congress. This is surely the most ironical provision in the entire Constitution.

[2] James Baldwin, *The Fire Next Time* (New York: Dial, 1963), p. 39.

order to be free. And some white citizens have found that they could not enjoy their own freedom until all became free.

There are those in our midst who want to perpetuate the bitter legacy of slavery. They reject the traditional ideals of equality and brotherhood.

One such group is the white supremacists. They are not confined to any one section of America. Sometimes they have stated openly their beliefs that they and their kind are superior, that colored people are ineradicably an inferior breed. At other times they have hidden behind the slogan of "separate but equal." In either case they have excluded citizens—often intelligent citizens of high purpose—from their associations. They have trampled on the rights, the economic ambitions, the educational aspirations of men and women, boys and girls. Sometimes they have unloosed terror in rural homes, city streets, even churches.

Another group has arisen to answer the white supremacists by making exactly the opposite case: black supremacy. The black supremacists assert that the white man cannot be trusted. They say that whites have always taken advantage of dark-skinned people and will continue to do so as long as they can. The white liberal, they argue, is as bad as the blatant racist: neither will play fair in the showdown. The black man, they say, is superior in morality, in sexuality, in racial vigor. As frustration and suffering have piled up, the black supremacists have grown in power.

The two groups—white supremacists and black supremacists —are radically opposed. One is trying to maintain traditional privileges; the other is reacting against oppression. The two groups resent, even despise, each other. But they have much in common. Both believe in racial superiority. Each is, in its own way, segregationist. Each believes that cooperation and equality are impossible. Each rejects "the American creed."

"The American creed" is a phrase used by Gunnar Myrdal in his famous book, *An American Dilemma*. Myrdal is the distinguished Swedish social scientist, who was invited to the United States to supervise a vast study of the racial problem. His monumental book was first published in 1944, then updated and republished in 1962. Its title refers to the conflict in American life between belief and practice.

Describing the American creed, Myrdal says:

> America, compared to every other country in Western civilization, large or small, has the *most explicitly expressed* system of general ideals in reference to human interrelations. This body of ideals is more widely understood and appreciated than similar ideals are anywhere else.[3]

The American creed, says Myrdal, "represents the national conscience."[4] Obviously Americans do not always live up to the ideals of the creed, but they know them and feel them. The ideals include the dignity of man and the rights of freedom, equality, and opportunity.

Myrdal finds three roots of this American creed. The first is the philosophy of the Enlightenment, arising in the period when the American nation took shape—a philosophy that put great value upon freedom, equality, and reason. The second is the Christian religion with its emphasis upon justice, generosity, and mutual helpfulness. The third is the English common law, which through many generations developed its principles of justice and equity.

It is too late in history to spend much effort giving an argument in favor of the American creed or the validity of racial justice. In this chapter I am assuming that all of us, in some way and to some extent, believe that a person should be appreciated for himself, not persecuted because of his race. But I am assuming also that all of us have some troubles living with our beliefs. Therefore I shall discuss three issues that trouble America in an era of national crisis.

HEARTS AND INSTITUTIONS

For the first issue let us examine a theme that is often expressed when race relations are under discussion. "If you want to overcome prejudice, you need to change the hearts of men, not

---

[3] Gunnar Myrdal, *An American Dilemma* (New York: Harper & Row, twentieth-anniversary edition, 1962; first published, 1944), p. 1.

[4] *Ibid.*, p. 23.

social institutions. And you should use persuasion rather than pressure." This is one concrete form of the argument about men and institutions that we began to look at in Chapter 5.

There are many opinions and many debates about this idea. Fortunately we do not have to rely upon opinions alone. The social sciences have studied the processes of social change and provide considerable evidence on the subject.

The common argument is that prejudice is something personal, that a person may overcome it in a kind of conversion, but that external social changes do not affect it. This contention is often especially persuasive among religious people, who are likely to emphasize the inner life of man. They may say, "You can't *make* men love each other. This comes only by changing their hearts."

Clearly there is *some* truth in the argument. It is impossible to buy love or to beat it into persons. No shuffling of institutions can make a reckless motorist love pedestrians. Institutions can, however, make him stop for traffic lights and thereby save some lives. The pedestrians will actually care less whether the motorist loves them than whether he avoids running them down. Similarly the Negro has sometimes said to the white oppressor, "I don't care whether you love me. I just want you to quit trampling on me."

Now let us go another step into the issue. Certainly it is plain that to *some* extent people pick up their prejudices from their environments. In certain settings it is extremely difficult for the white man to meet the Negro as an equal; in other situations it is relatively easy. People living in the two kinds of environment are bound to be influenced by them. Often the institutions of society mean that Negro and white never see each other in a social setting of mutual appreciation and friendliness. Then it becomes virtually impossible for them to become friends. It is almost hopeless to change the hearts of the two until they can know each other.

Social scientists sometimes say, "Behavioral change precedes attitudinal change." This (in somewhat colder language) is exactly the opposite of the common opinion that hearts must change before institutions can change. And there are facts to support the social scientists.

For example, the United States Army sought evidence on this question during World War II. At that time the army was segregated, but in emergencies some colored platoons were assigned to white companies. A sampling of white soldiers was polled to see how they liked the idea. In divisions where there were no Negro soldiers, 62 per cent of the white soldiers disliked the plan "very much." But among white soldiers in the mixed companies, only 7 per cent disliked the experience very much. Reversing the question, in the all-white divisions only 18 per cent thought it a "good idea" to have Negro platoons in the division. But in the companies that had Negro platoons, 64 per cent thought it a good idea.[5] Similarly public school desegregation, when well managed, has often reduced prejudice. The changes in social organization make possible new experiences, which change the attitudes of people. Institutions can change hearts.

But institutions themselves do not always change easily. In the case of the army, if the government had waited until a poll of white soldiers favored the change, the army would probably still be segregated. The change came because there was pressure for change.

There is a curious hypocrisy—usually so unconscious that it is almost innocent—in the widespread feeling that persuasion is right and pressure is wrong. What we overlook is that the people in power have been maintaining their position by pressure. They cannot consistently object if someone exerts pressure on them. Our generation has seen fantastic contradictions: dominant white people, who have kept their privileges through vicious coercion —including lynchings, educational exclusion, and a variety of economic weapons—have raised *moral* objections when Negroes used such pressures as legislation, court procedures, and disciplined nonviolent demonstrations.

It is doubtful that a power elite ever gives in without some

---

[5] Data from the Research Branch of the Information and Education Division, United States Army, reported by Gordon Allport, *The Nature of Prejudice* (Garden City, N.Y.: Doubleday Anchor Book, 1958; first published, 1954), pp. 264-265.

kind of pressure. I do not mean that people in power are always brutal cynics. They may want to do right. But they see issues from *their* perspective. Naturally they want to preserve old values, move cautiously, avoid any damage in the changeover. They are not highly sensitive to the pain of those who suffer injustice and cannot enjoy the values of the dominant group. Loving parents are reluctant to give freedom to children without some pressure from below. Benevolent despots rarely grant rights to their subjects without pressure. And moral white people, who do not themselves suffer the harshness of discrimination, are unlikely to act boldly until they feel pressure from those who do suffer.

Alfred North Whitehead once wrote: "It is the first step in sociological wisdom, to recognize that the major advances in civilization are processes which all but wreck the societies in which they occur."[6] I hope that is not true, but I am afraid it is. Had Whitehead lived to see the agonies of America's current racial crisis, he would no doubt have felt his judgment vindicated.

Of course there are evil uses of pressure. There is pressure that hurts the opponent and harms the very cause one struggles for. The amazing thing about the Negro protests of our time is their remarkable restraint and discipline under great provocation. Leaders like Martin Luther King, Jr., have been notable for greatness of spirit and ability to influence vast popular movements. White men in the power structure would have been wise to give far more support to these disciplined movements and their leaders. White resistance to legitimate demands of Negroes gave the opening to less responsible leaders. Hence it is not surprising that frustration and resentment have on occasion produced riots and wanton destruction. With valid protests have come inexcusable acts. Negroes are not better than white people, even though they have often had a better cause. Negroes are capable of the same wisdom and folly, the same nobility and viciousness as whites. But with all the talk about a "white backlash" against the acts of angry Negroes, we should recognize that Negroes are acting out their own "black backlash" against long oppression.

[6] Alfred North Whitehead, *Symbolism, Its Meaning and Effect* (New York: Macmillan, 1927, p. 88.

The answer to our troubles is not to forget about institutions, not to go back to working solely on the hearts of men. It is to recognize that man is a social being, whose life involves both his personal freedom and his institutional relationships.

THE RESPONSIBILITY OF THE CHURCH

As a second issue, let us look at the relation of the church to prejudice and discrimination. If anywhere the hearts of men are bringing about change, we might expect it to be here. But immediately we find a baffling, dismaying picture.

The data are complex. Gordon Allport, the Harvard psychologist, has summarized the matter well:

> The role of religion is paradoxical. It makes prejudice and it unmakes prejudice. . . . Churchgoers are more prejudiced than the average; they are also less prejudiced than the average." [7]

Let us start by looking at the church as a stronghold of segregation. In the days of slavery many churchmen tried to prove from the Bible that God endorsed slavery. Nobody quite argues that way any more, but some claim that God made one race superior or that God intended the the races to stay apart.

The most startling single fact about the practice of the church in America is that as late as 1946, about 90 per cent of Negro churchmen belonged to separate Negro denominations. The remaining 10 per cent belonged to denominations that were predominantly white, but the vast majority of these Negroes were in separate Negro congregations. About one-half of 1 per cent of Negro Protestants worshiped regularly with Christians of other races.[8]

Since that time many formerly white churches have welcomed Negroes into membership. There has been some development of genuinely interracial churches, especially in the inner city, and increasingly the big city churches are likely to have a few Negro members. But the number of Negroes involved is

[7] Gordon Allport, *The Nature of Prejudice*, p. 143.

[8] "The Churches and Segregation" (New York: National Council of the Churches, 1952). The figures were taken from a study by Frank Loescher.

statistically small, and the figures of 1946 probably do not require major revision.

We know that it is often easier to desegregate a school, a baseball team, or a factory than a church. Some churches will welcome a Negro and pay him to sweep the floor, but will turn him away if he comes to worship. The record of the church is so bad, both in its own life and in its impact upon American society, that Dr. Kyle Haselden, editor of *The Christian Century* and a Christian minister, has written: "Religion more than any other single influence has given racial injustice its abiding power." [9]

Now, without taking any of the sting out of that indictment, we must look at the other side of the story. Although far too slow, the churches made their convictions clear years before the Supreme Court decision of 1954, which awakened America to the fallacy of the old "separate but equal" doctrine. The National Council of Churches has been on record since 1946 as committed to "work for a non-segregated church and a non-segregated society." The major denominations have taken comparable stands. Christian leaders, both national and local, are making concerted efforts to rid the church of segregation. And churches are becoming racially integrated because of the convictions of their members—quite apart from the legal or economic pressures that are effective in other areas of public life. Protestants, Roman Catholics, and Jews have frequently united to work for racial justice.

Many leaders in the movement for racial equality have come from the churches. In the period of sit-ins and freedom-rides the public grew familiar with newspaper pictures of clergymen, white and colored, being arrested as they tested local segregationist laws and customs.

When the United States Senate broke the filibuster and passed civil rights legislation in the summer of 1964, Senator Richard B. Russell, leader of the defeated opposition, attributed his failure in large part to the clergy. And William Shannon, a newspaperman, gave a share of the credit to the theological stu-

[9] Kyle Haselden, *The Racial Problem in Christian Perspective* (New York: Harper & Row, 1959), p. 63.

dents' vigil for civil rights, a silent witness that continued 24 hours a day for many weeks in front of the Lincoln Memorial in Washington, D.C.

How can we account for the divided mind of a church which is apparently both more prejudiced and less prejudiced than the society at large? An interesting answer comes from some recent studies of the subject. The research has been done by investigators, who go into a normal American community and use refined techniques of interviewing in order to study the people.

The interviewers discover the typical prejudices of the area (since every area has its prejudices). Then they correlate participation in the life of the church with the prevailing prejudices. They are likely to find that the church members are *more* prejudiced than the nonmembers. Those who occasionally go to church are a little more prejudiced than those who never go. Those who go rather often are still more prejudiced. A pattern begins to shape up: the more people participate in church, the more they share in the prejudices of the community—up to a point. Then the pattern reverses. Increased church activity comes to mean lessened prejudice. The members most deeply involved in the church are less prejudiced than the nominal members or than the outsiders.[10]

There is one explanation that makes sense of these conflicting facts. In a society where churchgoing is a more or less accepted pattern of life, many people participate in the church simply as part of their "belonging" in the community. They are the conformists, so they share the community's prejudices more than the nonconformists who stay away from church. Increased conformity, increased church attendance, increased prejudice— all go together. People are using the church—as people have always used religion—to reinforce their feelings and desires, even though this requires them to distort the faith of the church.

But then comes a break in the pattern. The more fully committed members, who enter deeply into the worship and work of

---

[10] This general pattern has been found in many studies. I have here used specifically the report by Robert W. Friedrichs, "Christians and Residential Exclusion: an Empirical Study of a Northern Dilemma," *The Journal of Social Issues*, Vol. 15, No. 4 (1959), pp. 14-23.

the church, are likely to find their faith reshaping their lives and overcoming their prejudices.

The evidence, both in its troubling and in its hopeful aspects, might lead many a church to re-evaluate its program and many a churchman to think through the meaning of his faith.

A PERSONAL ISSUE

Let us look at a third issue: What can a person do to overcome his prejudices? Every person has prejudices of some kind, deep or trivial. Sometimes he is surprised to discover them. He may wish to get rid of them but they will not just brush off. What can he do?

When Robert Penn Warren, the poet and novelist, revisited his native Southland, he heard a woman say: "I think it's a moral question, and I suffer, but I can't feel the same way about a Negro as a white person. It's born in me. But I pray I'll change."[11]

This woman has a great asset in her struggle—honesty. She may not win, but she has a good start. She is far better off than those who bury their prejudices where they cannot get at them and then pretend to themselves that they have none, or than those who try to justify their prejudices by false science and corrupt religion.

Even so, overcoming prejudice is not easy. The answer is not simply *trying*. Some things we can do by discipline and effort. We can sometimes force ourselves to be more just to other people. But we cannot get rid of prejudice by effort, even by honest, determined effort.

However, we can do something about our prejudices, especially if we understand them. The woman described by Warren was mistaken in thinking prejudice was born in her. Perhaps she was indoctrinated from childhood with misinformation and the habits of prejudice. Or perhaps she simply absorbed prejudice from her environment. Or maybe she is clinging to her prejudice because it seems to fill some need in her life. If she can find the reason for her prejudice, she will gain something. The same

[11] Robert Penn Warren, *Segregation: The Inner Conflict in the South* (New York: Random House, 1956), p. 103.

holds for all of us, because—I repeat—we all have prejudices, though not necessarily racial prejudices.

Some prejudices are soaked up from the society around us. They have become habits, persistent but not very important to us, excess baggage that we carry around. It is surprisingly easy to get over this kind of prejudice, even though it seems to be "born" in us. All a person needs to do is to make some friends among the group that he has scorned. In some social settings this is hard to do, and we are driven back to the need for institutional change. But when a person associates with others, even though he has long been prejudiced against them, the normal processes of friendship can dissolve prejudice with amazing speed.

But another kind of prejudice is much harder to overcome. It is the prejudice that is part of our personal or group security system. If we enjoy unjust privileges because we are holding others down, then we are afraid to see justice come. Perhaps more often we are simply insecure persons, trying to overcome our anxiety and fear by asserting superiority over somebody else. (This is probably the most common reason for prejudice.) Then prejudice is like a narcotic; it does not help us, but we cannot get along without it. In such cases we will not overcome prejudice without at least beginning to get over our insecurity. We need healing.

There is no mechanism for conquering insecurity. That is why the language of faith talks about the mystery of the grace of God. But there are steps we can take. One step is to enter into the life of a group of people who share a common faith and a common commitment. There healing begins to overcome insecurity, and the need for prejudice disappears. Then we can seek friends among those whom we have despised, and our prejudices slip away.

MORAL CRISIS AND OPPORTUNITY

Gunnar Myrdal, in the book mentioned earlier, did one especially surprising thing. He was invited to come to America for the specific purpose of studying the racial problem. Since he was a distinguished social scientist, he might have concentrated on the economic, political, and sociological aspects of the issue. He did, in fact, give all these serious attention. But his major theme was that the racial problem is a moral problem for America.

By this he did not mean that he, as an outsider, was delivering the verdict that the problem is moral. He meant that for Americans themselves the racial issue is a moral issue. Here are his words:

> It is as a moral issue that this problem presents itself in the daily life of ordinary people; it is as a moral issue that they brood over it in their thoughtful moments. It is in terms of conflicting moral valuations that it is discussed in church and school, in the family circle, in the workshop, on the street corner, as well as in the press, over the radio, in trade union meetings, in the state legislatures, the Congress and the Supreme Court.[12]

When people face a moral issue, they sometimes assume that they must decide between their pleasant preference and their grim duty. But that is a curious way to look at morality. The moral choice, rightly understood, may be an opportunity. The pain of racial antagonism is deep enough that the American nation will not resolve its problems without more suffering; but beyond the suffering is a life better than any of us have yet known. The answer to conflict is reconciliation, and reconciliation is something to rejoice over.

Race has long been a moral issue for America. In her early history Thomas Jefferson wrote, "I tremble for my country when I reflect that God is just." We—Americans—have had past occasions of trembling over the racial issue; now, a century after the Civil War, we live in another time of trembling. We could crack up on the issue of race. We could lose our national unity and the respect of the world. But if we rise to the occasion, we may rediscover our neighbors—and ourselves. We may find that human brotherhood is less an obligation that we must strain to achieve than an opportunity that we are privileged to enjoy.

[12] Gunnar Myrdal, *An American Dilemma* (1962 ed.), p. lxxiv.

8 | Law in a Changing Society

AMERICANS OFTEN MAINTAIN that theirs is a government of laws, not of men. By this they do not mean that laws are more important than people. They mean that people are so important that *all* deserve the protection of law, regardless of their power or status; that nobody is entitled to special privileges denied to others.

Obviously we could not have much of a society without law. Laws provide two of the essentials for people living together: order and justice. Without order, life would be unpredictable, chaotic, capricious. No one would be safe or secure. Without justice, some would trample on the rights of others.

Justice does not "just happen." Human life is full of impulses that threaten justice. Every society has people who want to take advantage of others. Each person sometimes needs protection against others who might harm him. And every one of us, it is important to realize, needs some restraints lest he infringe on the rights of others.

For these reasons courts occupy their important place in civilized life. Throughout history tyrants have tried to dominate or corrupt the judicial process. And leaders in the cause of liberty and justice have always sought an independent and incorruptible judiciary.

Courts in the American system of government have strictly limited powers. They cannot legislate; that is the function of elected representatives of the people in town and city councils, state legislatures, and the federal Congress. Courts cannot initiate action to enforce laws; the executive branch of government has that function. The courts interpret and apply laws. When they carry out their responsibility, they preserve liberty and justice.

A strong judiciary, acting with integrity, has an impressive responsibility. Under the American system of separation of powers, it limits the acts of executives and legislatures. Congress and the President may dislike somebody, may think him hateful or guilty of wicked crimes, but they have no right to single him out for punishment. Every man has rights that no one has authority to infringe upon. If a man is unpopular, if he is a minority (even a minority of one), if he is wicked and mean, he is still entitled to "due process of law." The courts are the guardians of law and liberty.

Today, as sometimes in the past, controversy swirls around the courts, especially the Supreme Court. In 1964, Congress, raising the salaries of federal officials, specifically discriminated against the Supreme Court. Motorists riding through the countryside saw billboards calling for the impeachment of the Chief Justice. Partisans of various causes attacked the court about its decisions on racial segregation, religion in public schools, the rights of suspected criminals, and suspected groups (especially Communists).

Citizens always have a right to criticize the courts, which certainly are not infallible. But to understand the fury of criticism in recent years we need to look at the operation of law in society and its peculiar role in our time of social change.

THE SOCIAL SETTING OF LAW

A court does not operate in a vacuum. It works within a tradition and a legal system. And these are always the product of a history—in the American case, of a long and complex history.

Of course, all human societies have laws of one kind or another. Thinkers have sometimes tried to imagine what a completely lawless society would be like. The philosopher Thomas Hobbes said that without government the life of man would be "nasty, brutish, and short."

But if all societies have law and government, the nature of legal systems varies. In the United States the basic law of the land is set forth in the Constitution. There are both romantic and cynical interpretations of the Constitution. According to the romantic interpretation, the forefathers were heroes who struggled and suffered for the cause of freedom. After winning their cause, they enshrined their wisdom in a Constitution, which had the purpose of establishing justice and freedom. According to the cynical interpretation, the founding fathers were shrewd men who recognized what was to their own advantage and carefully devised a government to protect their interests.

Actually each interpretation is partially true—and each is incomplete. Men rarely see justice in any purity. They see what looks like justice to them in their particular position of privilege or need. So legal systems—unless they are sheer tyrannies—are set up with the purpose of expressing justice as the groups in power conceive justice. Almost any form of government reflects both the power structure of a society and the society's aspirations for justice.

The Constitution of the United States is no exception. From the beginning it was a great document of freedom—but the freedom it guaranteed was weighted on the side of special privilege. Its most monstrous flaw we have already noted in Chapter 7: it protected slavery, denied the slaves a vote, yet gave slave states extra representation in Congress because of the slaves. Even with so great an inconsistency, the Constitution expressed the cause of freedom so eloquently and firmly that citizens have looked to it constantly as a protection for their rights. Its authors were men of authentic wisdom, and they drafted more truly than they knew. Often their phrases have assured liberty to persons and groups whom they scarcely intended to help.

No part of this Constitution is more important than the Bill of Rights, spelled out in the first ten amendments. Here are the basic legal guarantees of freedom. Repeatedly when somebody or some group, with good intentions or bad, begins to infringe on the rights of others, the Bill of Rights protects the victims. It defines the rights of freedom of speech, of press, of religion, of petition and peaceable assembly; the right to trial by jury; the insistence upon due process of law. The courts are the guardians of these rights. Highest of all courts is the Supreme Court of the United States, whose nine justices have the awesome responsibility of upholding constitutional law, without regard to popularity or political pressures.

Foreigners sometimes wonder about American veneration for the Constitution. The British historian, D. W. Brogan, with friendly good humor has said that Americans worship the Constitution.[1] Gunnar Myrdal also has argued that sometimes "the American creed" is perverted into "worship of the Constitution."[2]

Actually, I think Americans do not, as a rule, worship the Constitution. In fact they often fail to give it its due importance. And always they know that improvements are possible, that changing times demand changing laws. The Constitution itself makes this clear when it provides methods for amending it. And the American people have amended it in 23 cases—or in 13 cases since the Bill of Rights.

It is important to American social life that the people, without worshiping the Constitution, respect it. Disrespect for constitutional government can threaten the whole structure of the common life.

THE CHANGING ROLE OF LAW

In our swiftly changing world the significance and function of law are changing too. One such change is the increasing importance of law.

In the American society formal laws have always had more importance than in most societies. Americans have been a diverse people expanding across a continent and constantly confronting new situations. They could not, like many societies, regulate conduct by traditions. Nor could they assume that everybody agreed upon the customary ways of doing things. In many human communities unwritten habits and customs govern behavior so effectively that few written laws are needed. The "common law," rising out of generally accepted practices, is more pervasive than "statutory law," enacted by legislatures. Unwritten constitutions

---

[1] D. W. Brogan, *The American Character* (New York: Vintage Books, 1956), pp. 18, 151.

[2] Gunnar Myrdal, *An American Dilemma* (New York: Harper & Row, 1962), p. 12.

have been as effective as signed and sealed documents. But Americans have found it advisable to place great emphasis on statutory law and a written Constitution.

The increasing pace and complexity of life has increased this tendency. In Chapter 5 we saw that the organized society requires a high degree of regulation. Individuals can no longer decide freely where they will make left turns, what they will do with the garbage, whether they will let their pets run around the neighborhood, how strong elevator cables should be, what radio frequencies they shall use, whether they will build a factory in a residential area. We make laws to deal with these and many other issues.

As the importance and scope of law increase, two other changes are taking place. Neither is entirely new, but both are new in scope.

First, law becomes increasingly a method for *changing* the behavior of people. Instead of maintaining established norms, it revises the norms and requires changed acts.

Americans have always believed that they could improve the society through good laws. But even so, laws have usually expressed the dominant opinions of the society—or of the power structure within it—against the dissenting few who preferred not to comply. Today the situation is sometimes quite different, most notably in the case of civil rights. Decisions of the Supreme Court and congressional legislation mean that, in some major local areas, the public law runs counter to the habits of the majority and the preference of the power structure. In some cases the law is actually changing the power structure.

From time to time power structures need to change, and almost always the established power structure resists the change. To bring about the change lawfully is a great achievement, far preferable to a violent revolution. It is not an easy achievement, as current history in America shows. Similarly to change by law the habitual practices of great numbers of people is not easy.

Therefore law has an unusual function in the transformation of American society. I am not saying that this function is unique or that it is bad. I am only saying that it is unusual and that it requires careful understanding.

Second, American society faces major problems of disobedience to law. We cannot measure the defiance of law; the only measurements are of *detected* violations. But most reports, federal and local, indicate a rising crime rate. Much of this crime centers in city slums; it is related to problems of poverty, lack of opportunity, and metropolitan pains that we have already noticed. But some recent indices show that the highest growth rate of crime and juvenile delinquency is in the suburbs.

Once again Gunnar Myrdal helps us to understand the issue. He has pointed to a curious paradox in this society. "Americans," he writes, "are accustomed to inscribe their ideals in laws." More than most peoples Americans try to meet social problems through legislation. They hear of some evil and say, "There ought to be a law against that." Yet, continues Myrdal, Americans are more ready than most people to set their private judgment against law and to disobey a law that they dislike. There is an "anarchistic tendency in America's legal culture."[3]

The social upheavals of the present time intensify the tendency. The causes of crime and delinquency are so complex that no one understands them entirely. But certainly they are related to the changes in established patterns of life, the dislocations of life and work, the upheavals in social relations—the various evolutions and revolutions that are the subject of this book. They require the best methods of research into behavior and the development of new forms of social organization that will make possible humane ways of life in this new contemporary civilization.

One other form of disobedience of law requires special attention. It is connected with the struggle for civil rights. Those who resent extension of civil rights have opposed law in ways ranging from the "massive resistance" advocated by prominent leaders to the murder of civil rights workers and the dynamiting of homes and churches. On the other side of the struggle, conduct has covered a spectrum from riots and looting to disciplined, nonviolent civil disobedience. Obviously not all these many acts can be lumped as law-defiance. Some careful distinctions are necessary.

In looking at the changing role of law we have raised two questions. Noting the use of law to overturn old habits and prac-

[3] *Ibid.*, pp. 14, 16.

tices, we meet the question: To what extent can law change behavior? Looking at the issue of disobedience of law, we must ask: When is it justifiable to disobey? Let us take up these questions in turn.

LAW AND BEHAVIOR

A good starting place to consider the first question is one of the favorite slogans of American life, "You can't legislate morality." Despite its conflict with the slogan we noticed earlier—"There ought to be a law"—it has great currency. As it is generally used, it is one of those half-truths that do as much to confuse as to clarify thinking. The complex relation between law and moral behavior is similar to the relation, which we examined in the preceding chapter, between institutions and inner attitudes.

The familiar slogan is persuasive because it includes an element of utterly convincing truth. Certainly we cannot legislate all morality. No law will force a man to love his neighbor or to forgive his enemy. No law will make him generous or compel him to show good will. Any high morality requires voluntary action carried out in a free spirit—action of individuals and of groups.

But the slogan includes an equally obvious error. To some extent we *can* legislate morality, and we *do* so all the time. There are ancient moral commandments—thou shalt not kill, thou shalt not steal—that have been made public laws. Although law cannot require a man to appreciate his neighbor, law can tell him not to kill his neighbor or to steal from his neighbor. Law can prevent men from forbidding their neighbors to vote. When laws have been inflicting injustice, a change in the laws is necessary to redress the injustice.

Laws are more effective when a spirit of public morality supports them. But sometimes law tells a man, "Whether you like it or not, you must do some things and you must not do other things." As a matter of fact, there is not much to legislate about *except* morality. Some laws are procedural or informative: even a society of perfect people would need traffic rules. But it is immorality that makes necessary the coercive element in laws.

Because men are not entirely moral, law must require them to behave with some regard for the public good.

In 1962, Earl Warren, Chief Justice of the United States, on the occasion when he was honored with the Louis Marshall Award of the Jewish Theological Seminary of America, made an address on the relation between law and ethics. Three themes in that address help to clarify the issues involved in legislating morality.

First, the Chief Justice pointed out that effective law depends upon moral awareness and commitment in society. Here are his words:

> In civilized life, Law floats in a sea of Ethics. . . . Without ethical understanding, the Law, as a Ship of State, would be stranded on dry land. When there is no ethical commitment to observe the Law, the judicial and police systems are really helpless, and the Law often ceases to operate at all.

Here is the clear insistence that law is not a substitute for morality. It is impossible to compensate for ethical weakness by imposing laws. When society is basically weak, evil, or confused, it is not much help to say, "There ought to be a law . . ."

But the second theme points to a countertruth. Chief Justice Warren put it this way:

> Without Law, civilization could not exist, for there are always people who, in the conflict of human interest, ignore their responsibility to their fellow men.

That sentence points to the necessity to legislate morality. Voluntary acceptance of responsibilities is preferable to forced acceptance. But sometimes men must be required to do what they will not do by their own choice.

The third theme of the Chief Justice points to the ethical behavior that goes beyond law:

> If there were no sense of love in families, if there were no sense of loyalty, if friendship meant nothing, if we all, or any large proportion of us, were motivated only by avarice and greed, Society would collapse almost as completely as though it lacked Law. Not only does Law in civilized society presuppose ethical commitment; it presupposes the existence of a broad area of human

conduct controlled only by ethical norms and not subject to Law at all.

Here is the awareness of the ethic that goes beyond demands of the law. Public law cannot control motives, and motives are the real stuff of morality. The moral man, after he has complied with the law, will recognize further ethical responsibilities that can never be legislated.

We can summarize the three themes in three sentences. On the most basic level, morality underlies law. Then law comes to embody and enforce some of this morality. But finally there is always a morality beyond law, asking more than law can or has any right to ask.

We can easily see the practical meaning of these three levels of moral responsibility. Morality tells us that we should strive to give all people freedom, justice, and opportunity. Law can go part way to enforce this morality. It sets up public schools, taxing citizens in order to pay for them and requiring children to attend them. It enforces civil rights when privileged groups try to deny them. Then, when law has done what it can, morality goes still further. Through such groups as United Givers Funds, the Red Cross, and churches, we voluntarily seek to extend opportunity. Or in personal relations we offer friendship which no law can require.

An interesting example of the effect of law upon public morality has been reported by the well-known political columnists, Rowland Evans and Robert Novak. It describes the change in Birmingham, Alabama, from the "violence and murder" of 1963 to the remarkable "tranquillity of desegregation" of 1964. The columnists appreciate the intelligence and good will of civic leaders, but they give major credit to the law itself. The law protects those citizens who are willing to desegregate; it requires compliance from those who will not act voluntarily. Birmingham, the writers report, refutes the idea that progress comes by changing men's hearts; rather "new laws are what makes progress possible."[4]

[4] Rowland Evans and Robert Novak, "Birmingham—'Keeping Our Fingers Crossed,'" *The New Republic* (Aug. 8, 1964), pp. 17-18.

Human affairs are seldom simple, and no one theory accounts for everything. Unlike Birmingham, some other areas show the difficulty of changing prejudiced behavior by law. But decades of history have shown the difficulty of changing it *without* the pressure of law. Any adequate change requires both the morality that law can enforce and the morality of free and generous spirits in men.

THE MORAL DUTY TO OBEY—OR TO DISOBEY—LAW

The remaining question concerns obedience and disobedience to law. Almost everybody acknowledges at least some duty to obey law. Almost everybody can think of circumstances that would justify disobedience or neglect of a specific law.

Let us start with the obvious. Law and order are precious achievements. Frequently they are not appreciated until a community moves to the edge of terror or chaos. Although all legal systems are imperfect, due process of law is certainly better than the uncontrolled play of power. Hence the individual who resents legal restraints has no moral right to capricious defiance of law. In Western civilization a long Christian tradition has enjoined obedience to law, even under a wicked or pagan government; and most political philosophies have assumed the importance of obedience.

But equally obvious is the fact that laws may be unjust and tyrannical. The Nazis, to take a plain example, made vicious laws that destroyed persons and social values. Today we honor courageous men who defied the Nazi government not for their own advantage but for justice.

The tradition of honorable disobedience of law runs deep in our society. Socrates went to his death saying, "Men of Athens, I honor and love you. But I shall obey God rather than you."[5] Peter and his friends in Jerusalem, when commanded to stop preaching, answered, "We must obey God rather than men" (Acts 5:29).

These are thrilling episodes in the history of mankind. But they raise difficult questions. Any malcontent can claim that God is on his side. What happens if each individual sets himself up as

[5] Plato, *Apology,* 29.

the judge of right and wrong, obeying or disobeying law as he chooses? The result may easily be social chaos, the breakdown of law, the risk of mob rule or lynch law, intolerable cruelty and injustice. Any system of social morality must require individuals, at least sometimes, to subject their own judgments to governmental authority.

Somehow men and women of integrity must avoid either the absolutizing of law as the final good or the exaggerated individualism that breeds contempt for law. Within the normal confusion of human affairs we cannot expect to find a perfect set of criteria to determine when disobedience is justifiable. But I suggest three situations when disobedience may be a valid choice.

1. The processes of constitutional government in the United States provide methods for testing laws in courts. Sometimes a person may believe that a specific law is itself illegal, that is, unconstitutional. Or he may believe that the orders of a particular government official are illegal. Then open, honest disobedience is a method of getting the case into court. The man who challenges the law in this way is not trying to cheat and is not showing disrespect for legal processes. His act may lead the court to strike down an unconstitutional law.

Many constitutional freedoms have been made secure because men risked disobedience of law in order to get a judicial judgment on the law itself. A famous case concerned James Joyce's *Ulysses*, now widely acknowledged as one of the world's great novels. For years the book was outlawed in the United States. When copies were imported, the customs authorities seized and burned them. In 1933, Random House, deliberately disobeying the law as it had been applied, published the book. In the trial that followed the United States District Court ruled that the book was not obscene and that the publisher could bring it out.

More recently citizens of Connecticut have wanted to challenge the constitutionality of laws against dissemination of information about birth control. They have opened clinics, which disobeyed the law. They expected arrest, and they wanted a judicial test of the law. Cases like these show respect, not defiance, for the legal system.

2. People may use disobedience to protest a law when it violates their consciences and they see no opportunity to change it. Normally, when one dislikes a law, he should work to repeal or to modify it rather than disobey it. Certainly in a functioning democracy the latter method is normally the right one. But if a tyranny or a corrupt bureaucracy makes orderly change impossible, some form of protest may become necessary. Or a minority with little influence may openly disobey a law and accept the consequences of its act, in order to impress the forces in power.

Thus America's forefathers issued the cry, "No taxation without representation." Patriots violated laws in order that they might win a right to participate in the making of laws.

Later in American history Henry David Thoreau, protesting the government's acts toward Mexico and the expansion of slavery, refused to pay his poll tax and went to jail. To his disappointment his friends paid his tax and the jailer turned him out. It is reported that Ralph Waldo Emerson, visiting Thoreau in jail, said in a shocked voice, "Henry, what are you doing in there?" Thoreau answered, "Waldo, what are *you* doing out there?" Note that Thoreau was not plotting to harm anybody and was committing no violence, trickery, or cheating. Society could see his act, invoke its penalty, and decide whether its laws were just.

More recently Negroes, often denied the right to vote, have disobeyed laws that they had no hand in making. In the most impressive cases they acted nonviolently, with superb discipline, in civil disobedience. They had the double aim: to challenge laws in court and to appeal to the conscience of the society. In some cases they won their tests in court; in other cases they persuaded society to change its laws.

3. In the two preceding types of disobedience the acts were entirely open and above-board. There was no plotting to harm other people, no basic disrespect for the legal system. The effort was not to evade a legal claim, but to challenge the law in the public arena.

A rarer type of situation may call for still more radical defiance of law. The case of a morally intolerable evil may drive people of integrity to conspiracies of disobedience.

Thus in American history the evil of Negro slavery led men of conscience to help slaves to escape via the "underground railway." Thus also the Nazi persecution of Jews led the best and bravest of men to disobey laws in order to save lives. Here the effort was not to make an open witness that might persuade the society to change; it was a simple, direct act to save persons from vicious laws. Any totalitarianism, whether ideological (like Nazism and Communism) or personal (like some in Latin America) may prompt similar acts of disobedience. In a government of gangsters an honest man is likely to be a lawbreaker.

Any of these justifications for disobedience to law may be misused as rationalizations for ethical irresponsibility. People are always glad for theories that will justify their own privileges and prejudices. But life requires us to take that risk. No rule, either of absolute obedience or of absolute individualism, will spare us the necessity to weigh the claims of personal integrity against the claims of society in those cases where the two conflict.

Responsibility, of course, does not end with the decision to obey or to disobey. The making and sustaining of laws is also a work of conscience. When laws are just, the valid reasons for disobedience are removed. And in an open society those who disagree with laws have the opportunity to work for their modification. A healthy society learns to cultivate respect for law, for the freedom of men under law, and for the rights of men to change law.

9 | Political Perplexities

IN A "government of the people, by the people, and for the people," politics is the business of everybody. The right to vote and to influence public affairs is a right won in America's national history by men who pledged "their lives, their fortunes, and their sacred honor" to achieve political independence and representative government. In the world of today political responsibility has become more complex, more far-reaching than ever before.

Long before modern times men gave serious thought to the issues of politics. The philosopher Aristotle in the fourth century B.C. wrote:

> Now, that man is more of a political animal than bees or any other gregarious animals is evident. . . . It is a characteristic of man that he alone has any sense of good and evil, of just and unjust, and the like, and the association of living beings who have this sense makes a family and a state.[1]

Ever since, Aristotle's words "political animal" have been used to describe man. People live in societies, like bees and many other creatures. But whereas the bees organize their society by instinct, men use their reason. They negotiate with each other in order to protect themselves or to assert their own interests. They change their social organizations from time to time, seeking to improve life. They can make far greater chaos than the bees, and they can achieve far more.

If man is always a political animal, he is not always so in the same way. In many societies politics is something that happens *to*

---

[1] Aristotle, *Politics*, 1253a (Oxford trans.).

people. But in other societies, including present-day America's, politics is something that people do. All of us are, or can be, in this operation. We are involved in many ways.

Every four years, for example, Americans hold national political conventions. Most people watch them on television. They are a combination of circus, revival, conspiracy, and deliberative assembly. After the conventions come the national campaigns, which are in part a sporting event something like the World Series and in part an appeal to the intelligence of the voters.

Politics reaches a fever pitch in America every fourth year, but it is part of life day in and day out. Politics is the art of government. Politics is the interplay of life with life in society, the body politic. It is the action of competing and cooperating human interests, the play of pressure and persuasion, the efforts of men to gain their own objectives and to improve the common life. More specifically politics means maintaining law, protecting citizens, operating courts; keeping up roads and public services; providing public schools; collecting taxes, paying social security benefits. The policeman walking his beat is put there by politics —not, we hope, in the wrong sense that he got his job for supporting the winning candidate, but in the right sense that he is appointed by lawful public authority. In modern society we are never far from the processes of politics.

This chapter considers some of the political perplexities and decisions in contemporary American political life. In discussing them, I shall first point out a paradox that has been with Americans throughout their history. Then I shall move to some issues arising out of contemporary social change.

AN AMERICAN PARADOX

The paradox started with the Pilgrims, who had so much to do with getting the United States under way. They believed firmly in God, and they believed that God should rule all of life. They wanted no nonsense about obeying God on Sunday and giving him the slip on Monday—or about practicing religion in church and leaving it there if it interfered with making a quick profit outside.

There was an admirable sincerity in this puritan faith of the early New Englanders. There was also a serious problem in it. These puritans were confident that they knew the will of God, and they were determined that everybody should obey it. They allowed little place for disagreement on personal morality or public policy. Anybody who disagreed with them was likely to be accused of disagreeing with God.

This theory of government is called theocracy, the belief that God is the ruler. The trouble was that men, not God, actually ran the government. And though these men knew they were not God, they did not like to have their political opponents insist upon the distinction. The practical problem with a theocracy is that it tends to enforce on everybody the religious and moral standards of those in power.

America long ago abandoned the puritan theology and political philosophy. But, as we shall see, the old tradition still exerts influence.

Much later in American history a very different religious movement took hold. It expanded in the eighteenth and nineteenth centuries. It was far more individualistic than puritanism. It emphasized the experience of conversion and the inner life of the believer. It has sometimes been called pietism.[2]

Often this inward, individualistic faith spread through the revivals that swept across the land, especially on the advancing western frontier. The man who "got religion" at a revival was expected to show the results in his behavior. He was supposed to shake his bad habits and live like a decent churchman. Personal piety and personal morality were the important things.

The revivalists—with the exception of some who boldly opposed slavery—had rather little interest in public life. They were inclined to separate religion and politics, as no puritan had ever done. Sometimes they took a rather dim view of politics, as an activity that called for compromises and deals that were beneath the morality of the good man.

The strange outcome in American history was that these two movements got mixed up in the national consciousness and have

---

[2] Pietism may be used to refer to a much more specific religious movement, originating in Germany and spreading to America. I am using the term in its broadest meaning to cover the beliefs and practices described above.

stayed mixed up to this day. If you scratch an American—whether he thinks he is religious or not—you never know whether he will respond as a puritan or as a pietist. As we saw in the previous chapter, he may respond to evil by saying, "There ought to be a law against that" (a puritan response). Or he may say, "Let's not get religion mixed up in politics" (a pietistic response).

Of course, a person might logically use both slogans on different occasions. Some bad situations can be corrected by law, and some cannot. The trouble is that people are likely to pick their slogans to fit their prejudices and their convenience. In recent years some have argued that the government should sponsor prayers in the public schools, but should not act to assure equal civil rights to all citizens. Such a stand involves a curious logic. Prayer would seem to be more an area for voluntary, personal decision than civil rights, which are a matter of social and political justice. But in the paradoxical mingling of puritanism and pietism, almost any judgment can be expected in one situation or another.

PERSONALITIES AND ISSUES

The paradox of puritanism and pietism is inherited from the past. Some other perplexities are more recent. The transformations of modern life affect politics as they affect all institutions. Frequently the old styles of action and organization do not fit well the new social forces in a dynamic society. The result is political ineffectiveness and frustration.

As a first case in point, let us look into one characteristic of contemporary American politics. One result of a technological, highly organized, metropolitan society is that government affects persons increasingly; yet persons feel more remote from government.

We have already seen reasons for both sides of this statement. On the one hand, the complexity of society requires increased coordination and regulation of human activities. Government has to be concerned with water supplies, transportation, education, protection of consumers, housing, public health—anybody can add to this list—far more than in a simple society. In a society of big organizations, government too becomes big. It impinges constantly upon all of us. But, on the other hand, precisely because government is so big and complex, it seems remote. Each of us deals with many agencies of government and cannot possibly know them all or their administrators.

As a result our participation in government comes to seem unreal. "We the people" are a pretty vague group, who do not know each other well. More and more we tend to think of government as somebody "out there" instead of as ourselves organized for the common good.

Simultaneously the demands of speed and efficiency concentrate the making of decisions among a few people. To take the most important example in American life, the Constitution jealously reserves to Congress the right to declare war. But modern weapons mean that military decisions must be made swiftly. Since World War II, the last declared war, United States troops have been committed in many parts of the world by presidential action. Military experts say that there may never be another declared war; or if there is, Congress will declare the war well after the fighting has started. If even Congressmen feel "left out" of the decision-making, as often they complain that they do, ordinary citizens are bound to feel still more remote.

The issues of government, meanwhile, become so complex that many citizens give up trying to understand them. Almost everybody would like prosperity without inflation, but few even pretend to understand the intricate fiscal and monetary policies that influence the pace of the economy. Most people want both a powerful military force and peace, but few understand the complex deployment of weapons that affects the issue. The opinion polls, which are so prominent a part of American life, frequently show startling ignorance among the American people on the basic facts of politics.

In Chapter 3 I argued that affluence, by enabling all the people to acquire political information, could contribute to democracy. The worker on a 40-hour week, I said, could with reasonable effort get a comprehensive political education. But this result, in fact, is rather rare. Certainly the political education of the public reaches its peak during the campaigns leading to presidential elections. But even at such times, says one recent study of American politics, the number of voters who can distinguish between the stands adopted by the major national, parties on issues is "rarely larger than 30 per cent."[3]

When such is the case, the moral appeals to citizens to do their duty by getting out to vote are entirely too simple. How can anybody gain moral satisfaction from voting unless he understands the issues? It is no wonder that many people feel a futility about politics.

In at least one way, however, people feel closer to their government than in the past. Mass communications have made the highest officials of government familiar persons in every home. Television is especially important in this regard. Most citizens are likely to feel a more intimate relationship with the President of the United States than with their city councilman or representative to the state legislature. They may or may not recognize these local officials if they meet them on the street. But the live picture of the President is often in their living rooms. All of us, in fact, recognize his voice, his gestures, his facial expression, his idiosyncrasies. We constantly react to him in appreciation or disapproval. During an election campaign we compare him with his opponent.

All this leads to a curious phenomenon in the affairs of government. Most citizens are modest enough to admit that they do not understand complex issues of government well. But where is the person modest enough to admit that he is not a good judge of men? All of us constantly judge our public officials. The content of their arguments is less influential than their personal bearing and manner of speaking. We assume attitudes of trust or distrust, based on extremely slim evidence. What we are judging is too often an image carefully projected on a television screen. More than we realize we are influenced by lighting, by facial make-up, by the way in which a man uses notes or a prompting device that we cannot see, by his quickness in answering questions (even when deliberation might be a virtue).

In all this we are not entirely deceived. A man cannot stand

[3] Nelson W. Polsby and Aaron B. Wildavsky, *Presidential Elections* (New York: Scribners, 1964), p. 11.

under the exposure of mass communications, especially week after week, without disclosing something of his true character. All in all, we probably make better judgments because of television than we would make without it. But the response to the face on the screen is a poor substitute for an understanding of the issues.

David Riesman has described the way in which such personal qualities as warmth, glamour, and sincerity become more important to the electorate than competence. The most important of these qualities, we would probably all agree, is sincerity. Certainly we would not want our leaders to be insincere—at least toward us. But the sincerity that is judged, as Riesman points out, is a marketable quality, comparable to the sincerity that is credited to popular entertainers. Referring specifically to political contests, Riesman says: "Forced to choose between skill and sincerity, many in the audience prefer the latter. They are tolerant of bumbles and obvious ineptness if the leader tries hard."[4]

As Riesman further points out, sincerity is a considerably more complex feature to judge than competence. But all of us like to think we can judge it. Hence the political leader must learn to project sincerity. "Just because such a premium is put on sincerity, a premium is put on faking it."[5] I suppose nothing is less sincere than faking sincerity, but apparently it pays.

The question of issues and personalities has always been with us in politics. But some of the social changes in the contemporary world—notably the increasing complexity of issues and the power of mass media of communication—raise it to critical importance.

THE SYSTEM OF REPRESENTATION

A second urgent problem in American politics concerns less the habits and judgments of voters than one element in the system itself. Any representative government requires a method of

[4] David Riesman, *et al.*, *The Lonely Crowd* (Garden City, N.Y.: Doubleday Anchor Book, 1953), p. 226.
[5] *Ibid.*, p. 227.

representation. If the method fails to do justice to the rights and interests of the society, representative government can be as undemocratic as an oligarchy or a dictatorship.

The social changes of current history have put severe strains on the representative system of the United States. Two of those strains are on the way to solution; a third is not.

1. The first strain concerns the right of citizens to vote. The original Constitution, as we have seen, did not permit slaves to vote. Following the Civil War the Fifteenth Amendment to the Constitution provided that no citizen could be denied the vote because of "race, color, or previous condition of servitude." But a long series of efforts, including terror and trickery, has prevented Negroes in some areas from voting. The injustice is a great one, especially because the denial is most common in the areas where Negroes are most numerous and discrimination is most vicious. If Negroes in these places could vote, they could correct many of their other disadvantages. Although no state has a majority of Negroes, more than 150 counties have. To prevent them from voting is an outright mockery of representative government.

A series of court decisions and the Civil Rights Act of 1964 have gone far to reduce the injustice. In some places a Negro still risks physical danger if he tries to register and vote. Even more often he risks economic reprisals. Voting registrars use many tricks to prevent Negro registration. But the power of law and of federal government is on the side of the Negro voter. The pain and trouble are not over, but the way to a solution is clear.

2. Despite the dramatic urbanization of America the election districts, both for state legislatures and for the United States Congress, have often not kept pace with the movement of people. As a result rural districts with few people can often outvote city districts with far more people. In an especially unfair case one man in a state legislature has represented 935 times as many people as another.[6] A majority of state senators might come from a mere 8 per cent of the population (Nevada), a majority of

[6] In Vermont in 1962 the 38 people of Stratton had a representative, as did the 35,531 people of Burlington. *New York Times,* Apr. 1, 1962.

state representatives from 12 per cent (Vermont and Connecticut).[7]

For many years the problem seemed insoluble, because legislatures which were elected by a process that misrepresented the population were not eager to correct the system. But decisions of the Supreme Court are now requiring redistricting. The solution may take time, perhaps some compromises, but again the way is fairly plain.

3. There remains a problem inherent in the American method of representation. Every member of Congress is elected by the voters of a specific state or congressional district. Often those voters have local issues in mind and want their Senators and Representatives to serve their local interests. But the Congress enacts legislation that concerns the national interest and often the interests of the world. The abilities that get a man elected may not be the abilities that best serve the country.

Thus a man may vote on national defense policy with an eye primarily to arms contracts in his home town. Or he may vote on international trade policies with his main interest in employment and profits for a factory back home. Or he may, after winning a local election as a white supremacist, influence United States policies toward colored peoples in the United Nations.

Usually the diverse local interests might be expected to balance each other out in Congress so that a truly national interest would emerge, except for one problem. That is the committee system in Congress. As Congress has increased in size, more and more of its work has been done in committees. These committees and their chairmen have great power. Men win chairmanships through seniority, which may have nothing to do with ability. Those who can most easily acquire seniority are those who come from districts with well-entrenched political machines.

Thus a Senator or Congressman with no national stature may influence decisively the destiny of the nation. A provincially minded Congressman may have great power over appropriations that affect world peace and welfare. A man of narrow sympathies

[7] *Christian Science Monitor*, Mar. 14, 1963.

and little understanding of the modern world may become chairman of the House Rules Committee and exercise an arbitrary power over legislation in all fields.

The result is serious misrepresentation of the people in Congress. A man who is elected by one district and who could not conceivably be elected by the public at large becomes for practical purposes the representative of all on urgent issues. Unlike the other problems of representative government, this one is not on the way to solution. Occasionally someone calls for a reform of congressional methods, but little happens. This flaw in the congressional system is undoubtedly one major reason why Congress tends to be less effective and the Presidency more effective in meeting the problems of a world on the move.

RELIGION AND GOVERNMENT

One further issue that is taking new form because of modern social change is the relation between religion and government. A conspicuous part—though not the only part—of the issue is the relation between church and state.

The United States offers a curious picture with regard to this whole question. On the one hand, the country practices the rigorous separation of church and state. On the other hand, it indulges in more political religiosity than almost any other country. Moved by both of these impulses, Americans occasionally find themselves in strange situations. Citizens battle in court and out of court over whether students may pray in the schools, whether coins may bear the motto "In God We Trust," whether the pledge of allegiance to the flag may mention God. How did this situation arise?

Actually the words "separation of church and state" do not appear in the Constitution—and nobody knows precisely how to separate the two, just as nobody knows how to separate politics and economics. What the Constitution says, in the First Amendment of the Bill of Rights, is this: "Congress shall make no law respecting an establishment of religion or prohibiting the free exercise thereof." From the time of Jefferson the phrase "separation of church and state" has been used to describe this situation. Courts have ruled that the Fourteenth Amendment extends to the states the restriction that the First Amendment places on Congress.

In some countries a specific church is "established"—that is, given official status by the government. In America this has usually been regarded as undesirable in two ways: first, it means an unfair disadvantage to those who belong to other churches or to no church; second, it is not good even for the established church, which loses some of its freedom and independence.

In another respect Americans have separated the church from politics. Some European countries, even where there is no established church, have political parties with the word "Christian" in the title. Such parties are usually related loosely to a specific church. A Christian party would not be illegal in America, but it is not characteristic of American politics. From the viewpoint of the churches a "Christian" party has three disadvantages: (1) it is bad theology to drape the mantle of Christianity over a political movement that inevitably rises out of many varied motives; (2) it is better to have churchmen exercising their influence in various parties, particularly the two major parties in a two-party system; (3) it is good for Christians to work alongside people of various faiths, cooperating and learning from many sources.

The separation of church and state, although traditional in the United States, has become much sharper in recent years than ever before. Throughout most of the history of the country the Supreme Court never issued a decision on this question. In recent years it has issued many. The reason is the increasing recognition that America is a pluralistic country—that is, a country of several faiths. Earlier, although no church was established, Protestantism was unofficially almost an established religion. Although a minority of people were church members, the chief opinion-makers were Protestants. Schools, legislatures, and courts operated in a vaguely Protestant atmosphere.

But changing patterns of immigration and cultural developments brought more variety. Catholic, Jewish, and agnostic groups grew in size or asserted themselves more vigorously. What had seemed to many people to be a nonsectarian Protestant piety turned out to be statistically one faith among others. It was not entitled to a monopoly of the public communications. It could not be established, officially or unofficially.

Hence the separation of church and state has taken a more rigorous form than in the past. Some common practices of the past, most notably devotional exercises in the public schools, are now prohibited. Many prominent Protestant spokesmen have publicly approved the changes, for both political and religious reasons. But many people have been disturbed by the change.

In spite of this increasing separation, the political leaders have been paying great deference to religion. As a single example, at the inauguration of John F. Kennedy as President, four clergymen were on the platform, and each was called on for a prayer. The total time spent in prayers was considerably greater than the time taken by the President's inaugural address. The percentage of time given to prayer was greater at the inauguration than in most church services.

Likewise most presidential addresses, especially on highly important occasions, refer (often in the last paragraph) to God. We hear a great deal of religious talk in high political circles. Some of the most devout people think there is too much. After all, those who do not take God very seriously seldom mind if his name is used rather freely. Those who are most serious about God dislike hearing people talk about God unless they really mean what they say. A genuinely reverent believer does not like God's name used to decorate political oratory or to win public approval.

Of course, political speeches do not necessarily use God's name lightly. Abraham Lincoln in his Second Inaugural Address spoke of God with an authentic Christian insight. Undoubtedly some recent Presidents have spoken of God because they had a true sense of the crisis in which we live and of our need for humility, guidance, and strength.

We shall probably go on living for a while with this curious relation between church-state separation and public piety. We may learn to brush off some of the excess religious talk, saving reverent language for occasions of real reverence. But we are likely to feel some continuing conflict as long as we believe simultaneously that religious faith should affect public life and that freedom of religion is desirable in a pluralistic society.

Perhaps this is the kind of conflict that need not be resolved. Perhaps it is healthy to live with—provided we understand it rather than evade it.

THE FASCINATION OF POLITICS

Politics and political ethics are huge subjects. It has not been the aim of this chapter to survey these vast topics. I have simply selected a few issues in which the epochal social changes, described throughout this book, impinge upon politics and call for responses.

For many reasons politics has a perennial fascination for men. On the most superficial level it has the excitement and drama of sporting contests. On this level most people are interested in politics at least occasionally. But to enjoy the great American political "binge" each fourth year is not to contribute much to the social order. Politics, we have seen, requires attention to issues as well as to men. It is a year-round activity of citizens in a democracy. It demands continuous labor in local arenas as well as in the national spotlight.

Politics has a second fascination. It is the avenue on which many men seek power. As such, it is serious business. It is also dangerous business. Power is fundamental to human life; nothing gets done without power. Anyone with good aims ought to seek power to achieve them. But power, especially unrestrained power, can be a threat to human welfare. Politics is one method by which society assigns power, distributes power, and determines the uses of power.

A third fascination of politics is, indeed, the most fundamental of all. Politics is one of the major areas where high purposes and practical activities interact.

Aristotle, we have noted, wrote that man, because he has a sense of good and evil, forms political institutions. The great words of political history are words like "justice," "freedom," "equality." But politics is also a thoroughly practical business. It involves persuasion, negotiation, organization, getting out the vote, discovering what can actually be done, designing tactics to do it.

Ideals detached from practice are only dreams. Practice without high purposes is mean and grubby. The union of purpose and practice is the challenge of politics—as it is the challenge of so much of human life.

10 | This One World

OUR TANGLED WORLD is one world. Teachers have been harassed for saying so. Geography textbooks have been banned from schools for pointing out the fact. But to deny that this is one world is about as effective as to deny that the earth is round.

The one world, of course, is divided by many conflicts. We do not all talk the same language, figuratively or literally. We do not all love each other. Our interests vary, our minds fail to meet, our struggles threaten life constantly.

But we cannot ignore our oneness. Astronauts can circle this earth several times in a day. A "hot line" provides instant communication between Moscow and Washington. Acts in remote parts of the world affect our taxes, our safety, our way of life. A dispute between Israel and Arab neighbors, a revolution in Cuba, chaos in Central Africa, warfare in Southeast Asia—these involve our interests, our money, perhaps the lives of some of us and our children. All of us, whether we know each other or not, whether we like each other or not, face the common threat of annihilation.

DANGEROUS WORLD

Over the entire world today spreads an invisible umbrella—the umbrella of nuclear terror. Any city on any continent can disappear instantaneously in a mushroom cloud.

Some of the disturbing facts, although they have been widely publicized, are often forgotten, perhaps because people want to forget them. It is a fact that today one plane or one Polaris-armed submarine can release weapons with far more explosive power than all the weapons used by all the armies in World War II. It is a fact that the Soviet Union and the United States together have explosives equivalent to ten tons of TNT for every person on earth.

During the presidential campaign of 1964 Senator Barry Goldwater urged that military commanders be given the power to use nuclear weapons without specific approval from the President. When criticized for this position, he replied that he meant only small, "tactical" battlefield weapons, which he maintained were comparable to older, conventional arms. Then Robert McNamara, Secretary of Defense, answered: "The average tactical weapon in Europe has a yield five times the bomb that was dropped on Hiroshima."[1] Even the very "small" tactical weapons (like the Davy Crockett, which Goldwater had mentioned) have twice the power of the blockbusters used in World War II, plus the additional destructiveness of radioactivity.

Looking at the awesome possibilities ahead, McNamara said:

> A full-scale nuclear exchange between the United States and the Soviet Union, lasting less than one hour, would kill almost 100 million Americans—the equivalent of over 300 World War II's. There would be little comfort in knowing that over 100 million Russians would also be killed.

The danger, already terrible enough, is likely to increase. As of this writing five countries have nuclear weapons, but more will have them soon. Within 20 years many countries may acquire them.[2]

In such a world accidents can happen. One example gives a hint of what conceivably could happen. On November 25, 1959, at 4:52 A.M. a green light went out on a panel at the Strategic Air Command near Omaha, Nebraska. Within 12½ minutes at

---

[1] *New York Times*, Aug. 14, 1964.

[2] For a sober and sobering appraisal see Harrison Brown and James Real, *Community of Fear* (Santa Barbara, Calif.: Center for the Study of Democratic Institutions, 1960).

about 100 bases scattered over the world, 750 planes loaded with H-bombs taxied out to runways ready to go. They did not take off. Their commanders discovered that the light had gone out due to an overheated motor.

There is no need to exaggerate the danger. I am not implying that a stroke of luck saved the world. The American military system includes elaborate safeguards against accidents. Specialists have taken great precautions lest radar pick up a flight of geese somewhere and start the end of civilization. But no system of precautions can take the danger out of the world.

We have evidence that the leaders of the world understand that mankind lives in a new era of history. President Dwight D. Eisenhower was the first American President to warn the nation specifically. Addressing Congress in 1960, he said:

> With both sides of this divided world in possession of unbelievably destructive weapons, mankind approaches a state where mutual annihilation becomes a possibility. No other factor of today's world equals this in importance—it colors everything we say, plan and do.[3]

This realization surely is nonpartisan. Four years later President Lyndon B. Johnson made the same point:

> Once—once upon a time even large-scale wars could be waged without risking the end of civilization. But what was once upon a time is no longer so, because general war is impossible. In a matter of moments you can wipe out from 50 to 100 million of our adversaries or they can, in the same amount of time, wipe out 50 or 100 million of our people, taking half of our land, half of our population in a matter of an hour. So general war is impossible, and some alternatives are essential.[4]

The President did not mean that the "impossible" war could not happen; he meant that large-scale war had become an impossible choice for rational men.

Premier Nikita Khrushchev, although he often blustered, understood this danger too. He knew what war would do to his

[3] State of the Union Message, delivered Jan. 7, 1960. Reported in *New York Times*, Jan. 8, 1960.

[4] Address to Building and Construction Trades Department, A.F.L.–C.I.O., *New York Times*, Mar. 25, 1964.

land, and he made concessions for peace. He did not want to concede more than he had to, but he clearly did not want war. He ran into a major split with Red China on just this issue. "It is only a child or an idiot," he said, "who does not fear war." [5] His successors, although they have condemned Khrushchev harshly for many of his acts, have not criticized him for avoiding nuclear war. The men of power in the Kremlin remain hard to live with, but they are realists; they know the dangers that they and the entire world face.

This realization does not assure peace. One reason is that nations which do not understand the danger may soon have nuclear weapons. Another reason is that the nations that do see the danger are still engaged in a hazardous game. They do not trust each other, yet they dare not fight each other. They must maintain nuclear weapons, to prevent the opposition from using its nuclear weapons. Both sides threaten and bluff, even while they try to avoid war.

We may expect this uneasy situation to continue for a long time. We are not apt to attain safety or relaxation. Tension and risk will be part of life. But there are opportunities ahead.

OPPORTUNITIES

The event that everybody would like but that cannot be expected is a dramatic breakthrough to a secure peace. Talk about such hopes sometimes has the unfortunate effect of preventing people from looking at more real possibilities.

Thus a lot of energy in recent years has gone into proposals for complete disarmament. At times spokesmen for both the Soviet Union and the United States have pretended to favor such a program, provided the other side would really come through on it. But any negotiations on such a basis are mere shadow-boxing, because both sides know that neither one will undertake total disarmament. If a country totally disarms, somebody has said, a few men with spears and horses could take over its national capital. Certainly Russia, with its long Chinese border, is not going to disarm completely. Neither is the United States.

A less spectacular, but still dramatic goal that appeals to

[5] Speech in Hungary, *New York Herald Tribune*, Apr. 7, 1964.

many people is nuclear disarmament. But this will not take place either. The United States, for reasons that are convincing to its citizens, will not get rid of all nuclear weapons without an air-tight system of inspection. After all, if America had *no* nuclear weapons, any country that managed to conceal only a half-dozen nuclear bombs could terrorize the nation. The Soviet Union, for reasons that are convincing to it, will not allow any thorough system of inspection. Such inspection would be to the disadvantage of the weaker nuclear power, both by disclosing openly its weakness and by revealing its strategic sites. So the effort at a sweeping agreement is frustrated.

Occasionally someone urges that the United States make a grand gesture of disarmament in the hope of persuading the world to follow. But there is no chance of persuading the American public to try that procedure. And the public in this case is not wrong. The world would be no safer if military supremacy shifted from America to Russia, to China, or to the Arab countries. Furthermore, as long as America has great power, it can enter into the general bargaining for peace. If America should renounce power, it would have no more concessions to make in order to persuade others to give up something.

In dismissing these various possibilities for a grand solution to the world's danger I am not advocating pessimism. I am trying to concentrate on the useful things that can be done. Despite all the deep strains of our time the world is safer than it was some years ago and than people expected it to be by this time.

If we go back to the period between 1945 and 1950, we find that the people who knew the situation best were making two gloomy predictions that did *not* come true. (1) They expected that any serious local war would escalate into a nuclear war, because the great powers would use their most destructive weapons rather than accept defeat or stalemate. (2) They thought that in a time of crisis each side would feel an irresistible urge to strike the first blow with the aim of destroying the enemy's power to retaliate.

Since those predictions were made, we have experienced several conflicts (especially Korea, Algeria, the Congo, and

Vietnam) that by all past standards could be called major wars. And we have faced up to crises (especially Berlin and Cuba) that rank among the most perilous in history. But nobody used nuclear weapons or gave in to the urge to strike the devastating first blow.

Why have we managed to do better than expected? There are two major reasons. First, the leaders of the United States and the Soviet Union, as we have seen, understand the grave dangers and they move carefully. I do not mean that they sacrifice everything for the sake of peace, but they combine bold maneuvers with a healthy caution. Second, the United States, followed to some extent by the Soviet Union, has developed the "invulnerable counter-force." Nuclear weapons in hardened underground silos or in submarines moving through the oceans will not be destroyed by the first attack. Hence the first strike loses its great advantage; anyone who delivers it knows that he will be hit by the counterforce.

Thoughtful military leaders and nuclear scientists are constantly concerned with decisions that combine technical strategic factors with moral factors. Sometimes the matters are so complex that the public scarcely understands them. Often the men who make the decisions suffer attacks from demagogic politicians who want a policy of more bluster and threat. But to a remarkable degree the United States government has sought to maintain a rational policy.

Thus, while no master stroke of diplomacy is going to make the world safe, there are many opportunities for the responsible use of power. It is possible to combine strength with restraint. It is possible for a country to maintain a nuclear deterrent so that no one will want to attack that country, yet not use it to coerce others, even when the temptation is great. It is possible to negotiate, to maintain patience, to endure irritations without flying into a rage.

Although no one agreement will remove the threat of destruction, many smaller agreements can lower the anxiety quotient of the world. Such agreements may be formal, like the treaty banning nuclear tests in the atmosphere. They may be informal, like the successive announcements from the Soviet Union and the United States of certain small steps in the direction of arms control. Compared with the great danger that hangs over the world, such steps may seem trivial. But whenever they reduce fear and distrust even slightly, they make further steps possible. The opponents of such steps point out that each one of them involves some risk. What they forget is that these lesser risks must be balanced against the greater risks that we constantly take in maintaining the potentiality for war. A people who are ready to risk everything for war should be willing to risk something for peace.

Every delay of nuclear holocaust is a gain—*if* we use the time won for creative efforts to meet the problems of the world. We can, if we are willing, employ the time to build stable societies, to help weak economies, to strengthen the cause of freedom around the world. To accomplish such aims is to win allies, not simply in the cold war against Communism but in the total human struggle for a better world.

One set of opportunities before the United States is connected with its membership in the United Nations. The United Nations has its enemies in America. It has those who like it when it supports us and resent it when it does not. And it has those who unintentionally harm it by expecting it to achieve more than it possibly can.

The United Nations was established by 51 nations after World War II. Now it includes more than twice as many countries. They are big and small, powerful and weak. They include people of all colors and creeds, from lands with widely varying governments. Missing from its membership—as of this writing—is the most populous country in the world, the People's Republic of China, whose 6 or 7 hundred million people are about one-fifth of all mankind. The Chinese government has been arbitrary and violent enough that a case can be made for excluding it; and there is no evidence that it would accept membership responsibly. But the United Nations falls short of being genuinely a world organization as long as so large a part of the world remains outside.

The activities of the United Nations and its specialized agencies are far flung. It feeds hungry children, helps refugees, provides health services to the world, controls traffic in narcotics, gathers information on population and economics, promotes technical skills, advances science and culture, sponsors education. Best known of its organs are the General Assembly, sometimes called the town meeting of the world, and the Security Council, charged with maintaining peace.

The United Nations structure has built-in limitations. The Security Council is often paralyzed by the veto. It can act decisively only when the five permanent members are willing that it should act. Since the biggest troubles in world politics involve disagreements between the United States and the Soviet Union, the Security Council cannot step in and end these troubles. It can resolve lesser problems. And even in the greatest of disagreements, it is a forum where the great powers air disputes. The parties involved at least keep in communication—no small achievement—and in the effort to present as strong a case as possible they occasionally modify their positions.

The General Assembly has sometimes acted when the Security Council could not. There is no veto power within the General Assembly. Its principle of representation—one vote for each member state—involves some grave difficulties. The principle of equal representation for weak and strong alike has a democratic validity, when it concerns persons. When it concerns nations, it is less valid. A small minority of the people of the world can be a majority in the General Assembly; and the voting strength of the nation has no relation to its power and responsibility in carrying out decisions. The General Assembly has often functioned effectively—just as the United States Congress sometimes functions well despite the difficulties we have already noticed in its representative structure (see Chapter 9). But a more effective world organization of the future, whether a modified United Nations or something new, will need to work out a better method of representation.

The United Nations, living in the midst of great strains in international relations, has made remarkable achievements. It deserves the support of men of good will. It is not, however, a substitute for a country's sound foreign policy. America can encourage the United Nations to deal with some situations that it normally prefers to handle by unilateral action. But America no more solves an international problem by turning it over to the United Nations than it solves a national problem by turning it over to Congress. Americans are wise to strengthen the United Nations; but even so, as a voting nation within it, America must bring to it international policies and goals for consideration in the world arena.

As the strongest and wealthiest nation in the world, the United States has an overwhelming responsibility, both in the maintenance of the United Nations and in the constructive use of American powers. In nation after nation the situation of people depends upon United States economic and military policies. Political pundits have occasionally resented the concern of other nations in American politics, especially in presidential elections. "What business is it of theirs?" some people have asked with a snarl. The answer is that American politics is inevitably the concern of other countries because it affects them so much. Arnold Toynbee once expressed the anxieties of other nations, as they worried about America's international policies, when he said that they might well raise the cry, "No annihilation without representation."

Naturally Americans are not going to give other nations representation in American elections. But Americans can give them consideration in the formation of policies, and should do so. Even the most powerful nation in history is not lord and master of this world. Indeed part of America's claim to leadership is the claim to respect the freedom and legitimate interests of other peoples, to seek friends rather than satellites, to represent the cause of freedom and justice.

THE ADEQUACY OF AMERICA FOR LEADERSHIP

The twentieth century has suddenly thrown great burdens on the American people, who had little past training for their new task. Traditionally America largely minded its own business within the world. Its own business, except for occasional forays in Latin America and rarer ones in the Pacific, was mostly at home. In two great world wars the nation had committed itself deeply in international affairs, but it liked to regard these as exceptions. America considered it virtuous to avoid involvement, and the country was likely to make moral judgments on the "imperialist" countries whose interests ranged over the world. Actually the virtue was largely practical common sense; a people expanding across a rich, unexploited continent had little need to enter into the affairs of other nations except in exceptional cases.

Now the American nation finds itself obliged, without much preparation, to exert its influence in distant lands. Its planes and ships, sometimes even its infantry are active in far parts of the earth. It transports supplies, wields political influence, picks up bills in dozens of nations. There is scarcely a country in the world where America does not feel a stake in the course of events.

American leadership has adjusted quickly to the new responsibilities. This is not to claim that these leaders have always acted wisely. But clearly they recognize the new role of America in the world. Because the necessary decisions rest upon such complex issues, the American people are inclined to say that their leaders are the persons who must make decisions. In large part this judgment is accurate.

But in a democratic society the leaders, although they carry heavy responsibilities, can never solve everything. What they can do depends upon the intelligence and understanding of the citizens of the country.

At this point two characteristics of the American public raise difficulties. With all the education and skill that characterize this people, these two qualities make it hard for them to exercise international leadership as well as they might.

In the first place the American public loves to turn every conflict into a horse opera. It likes to label the hero and label the villain. Whatever the hero does is good, and whatever the villain does is bad. It is the business of the hero to lick the villain in a fight—a hard fight, preferably a fair fight, but certainly a fight.

One characteristic of a fight is that what is good for one fighter is bad for the other. Often we think of bargaining and negotiation in the same way: any time the other side gains we lose. But this is not accurate thinking. Some bargains are good for both sides. And the art of negotiating is the art of finding policies that benefit everybody. It is not always easy to develop such policies; hence negotiation requires strength, patience, and imagination. But surely the prevention of nuclear war is a benefit to the whole human race.

To get out of the horse-opera mentality is not to be soft on Communism or to be unrealistic about power. It is to recognize that the world needs skill as well as power. It is to ask ourselves the profound moral question of whether we sometimes need to change, just as we judge it important that other nations change.

This was the theme of one of the greatest of President Kennedy's addresses. Speaking at the commencement ceremony at the American University, Washington, D.C., less than six months before his death, he said:

> Some say that it is useless to speak of world peace or world law or world disarmament—and that it will be useless until the leaders of the Soviet Union adopt a more enlightened attitude. I hope they do. I believe we can help them to do it. But I also believe that we must reexamine our own attitude, as individuals and as a nation, for our attitude is as essential as theirs. And every graduate of this school, every thoughtful citizen who despairs of war and wishes to bring peace, should begin by looking inward—by examining his own attitude toward the possibilities of peace, toward the Soviet Union, toward the course of the cold war, and toward freedom and peace here at home.[6]

Those words express the opposite of the horse-opera mentality. They ask for a maturity that Americans rarely attain. But the demand is urgent. For as long as the public insists on turning international policy into a melodrama and regarding all negotiation as weakness, they increase the perils of life in a perilous world.

The second quality that often misleads the American public in understanding the contemporary world is, in view of America's national history, a strange characteristic. This country, although born of a revolution, finds it hard to understand the revolutionary spirit that is loose in the world today.

The reason, no doubt, is rather simple. We—Americans— have had our revolution. Now we are more or less content with

[6] John F. Kennedy, "Toward a Strategy of Peace," June 10, 1963 (Washington, D.C.: U. S. Government Printing Office, 1963).

things as they are. Those in the most favored positions are seldom eager for change.

But the facts of life in the modern world meet us with a burning intensity. One economist writes:

> Though the United States has only a little more than 9 per cent of the free world's population and 8 per cent of its area, its citizens consume nearly half of its materials. The per capita consumption of raw materials is roughly ten times as high as the rest of the free world.[7]

While the United States puzzles over its agricultural surpluses, many people within the country worry about expanding waistlines. But elsewhere 10,000 people a day die of starvation or malnutrition, and more than half the world lives in continuous hunger.

President Johnson, urging a reluctant nation to put about one-half of 1 per cent of its Gross National Product into foreign aid, used this illustration:

> The developing world would soon become a cauldron of violence, hatred and revolution without some assistance. How would you feel if you were a member of a family whose total income was less than $80 per year? Yet a majority of the people of the world have incomes of less than $80 a year.[8]

There are Americans who chortle every time foreign aid is cut. Some do not care that most of the world is hungry. But India cares. China, Africa, and South America care. And many citizens of the United States care.

The problem, I think, is not vicious selfishness among most of us. It is failure to wake up to the facts of our time. It is the complacency of the privileged, who are not in the mood for change.

The demand upon America is for far more than financial appropriations for foreign aid. The demand is for some under-

[7] James W. Kuhn, "Rapid Economic Change: Aspects and Problems," in *Christians Face Issues of High Moment in Our Changing Economy* (New York: National Council of Churches, 1962), p. 31.

[8] Press conference with editors and broadcasters, *New York Times*, Apr. 22, 1964.

standing of a world that is in a revolutionary mood. Obviously not all revolutions are good. Some are brutal, tyrannical, unjust. But much of the world is responding to a revolutionary call for racial justice, for self-determination, for a higher standard of living, for opportunity to participate in the directing of world history. If we of the United States, proud of our own revolutionary heritage, cannot appreciate the desires of people who cry for food and freedom, we are turning over a great opportunity to our opponents. There are other nations who know how to take advantage of the revolutionary spirit that moves through the world these days.

POLICY, ETHICS, AND FAITH

International policy is perplexing enough under any circumstances that it sometimes seems best not to complicate it further with too much consideration of ethics and of faith. For the most part nations act in terms of national interest—hopefully an enlightened national interest, but in any case their own interest. If they know this and know that other nations are acting for their own interests, they can assess a situation realistically and act rationally. When there are collisions of interest, compromises are desirable.

When ethics comes into the picture, compromise becomes harder. A nation usually assumes that its cause is right and its enemy's cause wrong; then compromise seems shameful. If religion is added to the picture, the conflict becomes still more intense. Holy wars are the most fanatical of all. When people become convinced that God is on their side, defeat of the enemy becomes sacred duty and compromise becomes disgrace.

For these reasons some of the most profoundly religious men are reluctant to bring their faith too prominently into decisions of international policy. It is wise to be suspicious of anybody who talks conspicuously about God and righteousness in international relations, especially if he wants to annihilate the enemy.

But ethics and faith cannot stay out of international problems, for the reason that they will not stay out of any important human concern. International problems are, in fact, moral problems. We can quickly grant that they are economic and military and psychological—they are never *solely* moral. But all of them have moral aspects.

Some, living by the slogan "All's fair in love and war," say there is no place for morality in war—hot or cold war. Admittedly it is not easy to be moral in international affairs. We expect our government to do things—spying, bribing, threatening, sometimes killing—that we would not do to our neighbors.

But if there is no morality in our struggle—in our aims and in our methods—we lose our self-respect and the respect of others. We can only struggle consistently and we can only ask the support of allies for a cause in which we believe. We can judge the profundity of our belief by asking whether it simply justifies our cause or whether it sometimes requires us to modify the cause.

Faith, although related intimately to morality, is always more than morality. It is peculiarly significant for life in a time of continuous crisis and danger like our own.

Crisis generally brings two opposite temptations. One is the temptation of futility that asks, "What's the use?" and quits trying. The other is the temptation of arrogance that assumes we can always have our way if we are only tough enough.

A more mature attitude than either of these was expressed by President Kennedy in that notable television conversation at the end of two years in office. When asked about his experiences in the presidency, he answered in conversational style:

> Well, in the first place, I think the problems are more difficult than I had imagined they were. Secondly, there's a limitation upon the ability of the United States to solve these problems. . . .
>
> I think our people get awfully impatient and, maybe fatigued and tired, and saying, "We've been carrying this burden for 17 years. Can we lay it down?" We can't lay it down, and I don't see how we are going to lay it down in this century.[9]

Those were wise words. They reach to the heart of action in crisis. Serious crisis requires that men bear burdens faithfully,

[9] Transcript of interview of Dec. 17, 1962, printed by the CBS Television Network.

even though they know their actions will not resolve their difficulties.

Our problem is that we live in a tangled world, where our impatience and frustration may lead to actions that snarl it still further. Any cheap morality or faith will serve us badly. Yet there is the possibility of living with the confidence that, although we cannot untangle this whole world, every act of generosity and courage is worthwhile.

11 | Revolution in Sexual Ethics

AS LONG AS HUMAN LIFE has existed, people have been men and women, boys and girls. They have exulted in their sexuality, resented it, worshiped it, abused it. They have wondered about its mystery. Because of its explosive energy and its creative power, they have seen in it a symbol. It has represented the kinship of man with cosmic power and with the fertility of nature. Sexuality has been part of many religions, the occasion for exploitation and cruelty, part of the shared life of man and woman in the family.

Sexuality is part of the distinctiveness of humanity. People sometimes think of it as part of their animal nature, and in some ways, of course, it is. It can erupt in a violence that defies human rationality. But sex in man is peculiarly human. In the animals it is controlled by instinct, given full expression at limited times and mating seasons. In humanity it is freed. Man, it is said, is the only animal who makes love all year round. For man and woman sex is never solely impulse. It is the expression of selfhood. The Book of Genesis in the Bible describes sex as God's creation, related to the image of God in man: "So God created man in his own image, in the image of God he created him: male and female he created them" (Gen. 1:27).

Today a major rethinking of sexuality is in process. Everywhere people are talking about the revolution in sexual ethics. Often they are wondering to what extent contemporary society is achieving a healthy appreciation of sex and to what extent it is asking for trouble.

To move from the discussion of economic, political, and international decisions to a consideration of sex may seem like taking a jump from the most public issues to the most intimately private matters. But the appearance is deceptive. Sex is never entirely a private question, because a person is never solely a private individual. He lives in his culture, and his culture lives in him. In sexual behavior as in the obviously public spheres are focused today the anxieties of modern man, the questioning of inherited traditions, the influence of new techniques upon old habits, and the continuous search for the meaning of our humanity.

HOW REVOLUTIONARY?

We do not know as much about the revolution in sexual ethics as some of us think we know. In dealing with affluence, race relations, or nuclear weapons we can define with some precision the new factors in the present situation. In the case of sexual behavior we are not nearly so sure.

Of course there are stacks of charts and statistical data about sex—in marriage, outside of marriage, before marriage. We know less about the meaning of the figures. Nobody can put on a chart the meaning of the love of two persons who have shared the joys and sorrows of life. And we know even less about behavior in the past. Former generations left no charts to be compared with ours. If we want to understand ourselves, shall we compare the behavior of people today with that of Don Juan or with the Puritans?

But if our information is incomplete, we have some facts. Dating practices have changed. We can read about the quaint customs of a century ago and compare them with the much freer practices today. We know also some of the things that happen outside the rules. Contemporary civilization, providing first the automobile and then the motel, has given youth possibilities that were not available a generation or two ago.

We know also that one motive for morality, not a high one but often a powerful one, has always been fear. Today the old sanctions—the threats of pregnancy and of venereal disease—are less fearful than they used to be. Even so, the rates of conceptions out of wedlock, of abortions, and of disease are high. In the United States more than 250,000 babies are born to unmarried mothers each year, and about 1 out of 5 brides is pregnant at her wedding.[1] Estimates of illegal abortions in the United States range from 200,000 to one million; perhaps 1 out of 4 pregnancies ends in abortion.[2]

We can recognize the change that has taken place in bookstores, movie theaters, and newsstands. It should be noted that some of the "daring" best-sellers are books written long ago; but whereas these books were once suppressed, they now are available publicly. Sometimes the change has meant freedom for publication of great works of art (as in the case of *Ulysses,* mentioned in Chapter 8); sometimes it has increased the output of literary trash.

Everybody recognizes that this is a time of widespread experimentation and rejection of old inhibitions. People sometimes forget that traditional morality has always been defied. A reading of Chaucer, Rabelais, and Shakespeare makes it clear that the moral codes were not obeyed by everybody. A society that knows the stories of David and Bathsheba, of Antony and Cleopatra, of Tristan and Isolde cannot regard sexual extravagance as a modern invention. But today surely there is more open rejection of old standards and more puzzled questioning among well-intentioned people than in much of the past.

The meaning of behavior, I have suggested, is harder to assess than the mere facts. So it is not easy to answer the question: How healthy is the American awareness of sex today?

Shall we agree with the English novelist, John Osborne, that

---

[1] Mary S. Calderone, M.D., *Western Journal of Surgery, Obstetrics and Gynecology,* Mar.-Apr., 1964.

[2] James Ridgeway, "One Million Abortions," *The New Republic,* Feb. 9, 1963.

America is a "sexual nuthouse"? Or with the anthropologist, Eric Dingwall (also an Englishman), who says that "the United States is almost, if not quite, the most sex-obsessed country in the world"? Or shall we take the judgment of Hugh Hefner that Americans are achieving a healthy enjoyment of life in rejecting the restraints of the past? Or shall we accept David Riesman's belief that American society is not notable for sexual energy or ambition, but that people without much sense of purpose look to sex as a "defense against the threat of total apathy," and for assurance that they are alive and are having the experiences they think other people are having?

Some people are sure they know the answers to queries like these. But when the answers are so diverse and contradictory, we are wise to question them all.

TWO INHERITED ATTITUDES

One way to get our bearings is to investigate some of the attitudes that we have inherited from the past. Man always interprets his experience against some background of memory and history. From the many themes of the past I shall, at the risk of great oversimplification, mention two here. Let us call the first the negative or repressive; the second, the affirmative or expressive.

It is remarkable to see how often people have taken a basically negative view of their own sexuality. Probably we could find some reasons for this. After all, undisciplined sexual activity has ruined a great many people. It has on occasion led to rape, murder, conspiracy, and folly. So some persons have wished they could be rid of the whole business.

This negative viewpoint has often—though certainly not always—pervaded Oriental philosophy and religion. Sages have seen sex as a temptation to be conquered, as a diversion of human energies from loftier goals. A modern representative of this thought was the great leader of India, Mahatma Gandhi.[3]

In the West many men in the ancient world sought to reject sex. Plato taught that the lusts of the body corrupt the purity of

[3] Mohandas K. Gandhi, *The Story of My Experiment with Truth* (Washington, D.C.: Public Affairs Press, 1948), especially Part 3, Chap. 7-8.

the soul and cause strife, pain, and misery.[4] In the sex-satiated atmosphere of Hellenistic–Roman society, men and women occasionally reacted with a desire to have done with all sexual activity. Some—not all—of the ancient and medieval monks shared this attitude. Puritanism and the Victorian ethic were more or less influenced by this negative judgment on sex.

Today, however, the affirmative or expressive attitude prevails. Our society likes to think of itself as modern and enlightened. Actually many of our attitudes are not particularly modern, but are as old as human nature. For example, Hollywood columnists are likely to describe an actress as a "sex goddess." In the past people frequently worshiped sex gods and goddesses— and in the worship sought to imitate them. The practices of some primitive tribes and some past civilizations are filled with examples.

In Western civilization the medieval troubadors glorified romantic love, usually illicit love, and the historic Don Juan began to become the legendary Don Juan. Then the Renaissance brought fame to many adventurers who delighted in their sexual conquests. Later, when Puritan and Victorian morality disciplined sexual expression, there were always rebels who defied the ethical norms. Although the Victorian era commonly stands for a stuffy conventionalism, any sampling of the historical evidence throws considerable doubt on the popular impression.

In the twentieth century the defiance of the established codes became widespread and open. It was most crude and explicit in Nazi Germany, where the cult of "healthy eroticism" encouraged behavior that increased the birth rate or pleased the soldier on furlough. In the United States today the sexual revolution is not that coarse and blatant. It preserves more of the romantic feeling, aspires to more sophistication.

We might sum up the changed situation by saying that an old slogan, "Beware of sex," has given way to a new slogan, "Hurrah for sex!" But if there are a few people for whom one slogan or the other is an adequate expression, there are many more who are caught in the change and are perplexed.

Since the second slogan is more in vogue than the first, let us

[4] Plato, *Phaedo,* 66-67.

look at it. I am as ready as the next person to say, "Hurrah for sex." Sex is real, important, wonderful. But to say, "Hurrah for sex" is only the beginning of an understanding of it. If one says, "Hurrah for life!" he must still decide what he will make of his life. To approve of sex is the starting point for deciding how to appreciate sex, how to enjoy and respect it, in oneself and in others.

PRESENT PERPLEXITIES

As a brief way of describing the present situation of our culture, in its search for the meaning of sexuality, I suggest six words. Any one of them is misleading if taken by itself. All six together are misleading if taken as a glib summary. But each word stands for a real aspect of contemporary life.

1. *Confusion.* Our society is not sure where we are or where we are going. A sampling of a month's newspapers will turn up controversial and conflicting items on such subjects as what high school students do after the dance, censorship of books and movies, abortion, divorce statistics, behavior in college dormitories, birth control and contraceptives, women's styles (one season it was topless bathing suits), the antics of famous movie stars, court rulings on legislation, appeals for new legislation. Participants in the public discussion include politicians, teachers, students, artists, journalists, clergymen. Participants in private discussions include almost everybody.

2. *Liberation.* Many of the old restraints and inhibitions are gone. Others, still lingering, are on the way out. People are trying to decide what to do with their freedom. Often the first response to new freedom is to reason, "Whatever has been forbidden must be worth trying." The second response may be to realize that the first response is not intelligent in any area outside of sex and may not be in sex. Eventually persons must seek to define freedom—freedom from the tyranny of peer groups as well as from convention, freedom from the slavery of impulse as well as of inhibition. Today's society, both a little excited and a little frightened by freedom, is seeking to learn its meaning.

3. *Commercialization.* There is money in sex. There always has been (as long as there has been money), but today's world

has invented new ways of commercializing sex. The old-fashioned selling of sex for money is on the decline; it is unsophisticated. Our society still cultivates some unsophisticated ways of making money from sex: pornography is reportedly a half-billion-dollar-a-year business. But far more lucrative is the deft use of sex by the "hidden persuaders" in the advertisements. The modern advertising industry has made marvelous discoveries, not about selling sex (an ancient discovery) but about using sex to sell practically everything.

4. *Mechanization.* A lot of sexual talk and activity these days is about as joyless and mechanical as driving a car through a traffic jam. A technical society has inevitably produced a huge literature on the techniques of sex. Some of the books are good, some poor. All of them mislead if they make people think that technique is a substitute for personal meaning. Psychologist Rollo May has commented: "When emphasis beyond a certain point is placed upon technique in sexuality, the person finds that he has separated himself all the more from . . . his own spontaneity and joy and the surging up of his own experience of potency."[5]

5. *Trivialization.* Strangely the very effort to enhance and enjoy sex has often robbed it of its power. Walter Lippmann asked the cogent question some years ago: "If you start with the belief that love is the pleasure of a moment, is it really surprising that it yields only a momentary pleasure?"[6] More recently David Boroff compared today's "younger generation" with an earlier younger generation by saying, "What was tense sexual melodrama twenty years ago seems to be little more than reflex action today."[7]

6. *Realization.* Sometimes in our society, as sometimes in man's long past, man and woman enter into a personal relation in which they realize the wonder and joy of sex. Such realization does not come through concentration on sex alone. The persons

[5] Rollo May, *Symbolism in Religion and Literature* (New York: George Braziller, 1960), p. 29.

[6] Walter Lippmann, *A Preface to Morals* (New York: Macmillan, 1929), p. 304.

[7] David Boroff, "Sex: The Quiet Revolution," *Esquire* (July, 1961), p. 96.

involved are concerned not simply for sex, but for each other.
Yet it is not enough that they dote on each other. They seek to
share life, to join together in work and joy and appreciation for
the mystery of life and love. Then sexual activity is one expression of mutuality and commitment.

It is one of the wonders of sex that flashes of this realization
may illumine even the more mechanized and trivialized relationships that are so common in our society. But the authentic, profound realization is rather rare in a society that often reveals a
hunger for it. And, of course, it is never totally untainted. Denis
de Rougemont has called marriage at its best "poise in imperfection." [8] The poise is the more wonderful as men and women
acknowledge their imperfection.

FAITHFUL LOVE

Contemporary society, involved in its revolution in sexual
ethics, is not likely to turn expectantly for understanding to the
Bible. But those who do so are often surprised at what they find.
This literature—which tells of polygamy, concubinage, lust and
adultery, asceticism, and much else—communicates also a powerful expression of the meaning of sex. The Bible brought its own
revolution in sexual ethics, a revolution often perverted and seldom understood even today.

The key passage, I think, is in the second chapter of Genesis.
This chapter tells about the creation of man and woman. Long
after it was written, Jesus quoted it to express his convictions
about the meaning of marriage.

As we look at the record, it is important to get one problem
out of the way immediately. We shall not find here a scientific
description of how the human race appeared on earth. The author has no intention of writing science. He tells a story that
expresses a belief that sexuality is a gift from God and the basis
of a profound human relationship. He does it with a magnificent
earthiness and a penetrating spirituality that are inseparable.

In Genesis 2:7 we read: "Then the Lord God formed man

[8] Denis de Rougemont, *Love in the Western World* (New York: Pantheon,
1956), p. 302.

of dust from the ground, and breathed into his nostrils the breath of life; and man became a living being." Notice that man is akin to nature—made of dust from the ground—and akin also to God, who gave him the breath of life. There is no hint here that man's body or his physical nature is bad. It is this body that becomes the living person when God gives it the breath of life.

The story goes on to tell how God placed man in the Garden of Eden. After a while it continues: "Then the Lord God said, 'It is not good that the man should be alone; I will make him a helper fit for him.' " Man alone, this record is saying, is lonely and incomplete. He needs a companion, a helper. Other men will not be adequate. The man needs another person, akin to him, yet different.

But before we get to the creation of woman, there is a delay. God creates the animals. Once again let us notice that this is not a scientific treatise. Science tells us that animals lived on earth before man. Another author, writing in the first chapter of Genesis, puts the creation of the fish, birds, and animals ahead of the creation of man. The second chapter makes a different point. The animals are related to man. They are made of the same stuff of the earth by the same God. Man sees them and gives them names. But, the account continues, "for the man there was not found a helper fit for him." The animals are not an adequate answer to man's loneliness.

Now we come to the great event: "So the Lord God caused a deep sleep to fall upon the man, and while he slept took one of his ribs and closed up its place with flesh; and the rib which the Lord God had taken from the man he made into a woman and brought her to the man."

Let us not get literal about that rib; if we do, we simply turn a sound insight into bad zoology. But see what the writer is getting at, as he continues: "Then the man said, 'This at last is bone of my bones, and flesh of my flesh; she shall be called Woman, because she was taken out of Man.' " Here is the joyful exclamation of the man. He has lived through the loneliness, first of solitude, then of life with the animals. Now "at last" he has found what he craved.

Then come two fascinating sentences. "Therefore a man leaves his father and his mother and cleaves to his wife, and they become one flesh. And the man and his wife were both naked, and were not ashamed."

In those exuberant sentences three things are worth noticing. First, the woman whom the man cleaves to becomes his wife. She is not a plaything to be enjoyed and then forgotten, not a convenience for the man's aggressiveness or lust, but a wife. Man leaves mother and father in order to cleave to her. Second, there is a wonderful eagerness in the way man and wife become one flesh. There is no false spirituality here, no apology for the physical, no shame over nakedness, but a glad acceptance of the physical union. Third, no mention is made at this point of children. That will come later. Children in the Bible are a blessing of marriage. The married couple often long for them. But the fleshly union of husband and wife need not be justified as a means to some other end. It is good of itself. It is part of God's purpose.

In that ancient story of creation is an appreciation of sex, in its freedom and its commitment, its delight and its seriousness, that has a fresh ring even in the jaded world of today. Some, of course, will argue that it is obsolete. But we can foolishly escape responsibilities and opportunities by calling them obsolete. Interestingly some of the most contemporary psychology, using a clinical rather than a poetic language, makes the same points.

A name that would rank high on any list of American psychologists and that would head some lists is Erik Erikson. He works, generally speaking, in the Freudian tradition, which many people would try to oppose to the biblical heritage. He describes six conditions that should be included in sexual mutuality. I list them in his language:

1. mutuality of orgasm
2. with a loved partner
3. of the other sex
4. with whom one is able and willing to share a mutual trust
5. and with whom one is able and willing to regulate the cycles of
   a. work

b. procreation
c. recreation
6. so as to secure to the offspring, too, a satisfactory development.[9]

Erikson points out that any such achievement, on a widespread basis, is more than an individual accomplishment. He adds that it is more than a sexual matter also.

Thus it is evident that a healthy outcome for the sexual revolution of the twentieth century requires far-reaching changes throughout the whole of our culture. If we would rise above the commercialization and trivialization of sex, we must build a society that appreciates persons rather than commercializing and trivializing them. If we would avoid the mechanization of sex, we must establish social relations that subordinate machines to human beings.

The various issues described, chapter by chapter, in this book are clearly not isolated issues. Substantial progress on any of them requires progress on all. But this does not mean that we must wait in frustration until we see a resolution of all the problems of mankind. It means rather that as we work on any one, we see its relation to the others.

Sex ethics presents issues on which every individual makes decisions. He may see nothing that he can do about unemployment or nuclear warfare, but he obviously is doing something about sex. He may even cultivate the illusion that sex is a private affair. As we have seen, it is as fully a cultural as it is an individual matter. But it is one issue for which persons can take some responsibility. Even in a society not notably friendly to the idea, many persons know the meaning of faithful love.

RECOVERY OR LOSS

There are many more things that might be said. I could elaborate on the temptations of sex, so obvious and yet so deceptive. I could observe that in an imperfect world no love is ever perfect and no transgression is beyond forgiveness. I could talk about how even marriage may be a temptation, as people avoid responsibilities for the sake of the comfort and security of the

[9] Erik Erikson, *Childhood and Society* (New York: W. W. Norton, 1950), pp. 230-231.

family. I could comment on the peculiar concentration and devotion of many men and women who have not married.

But in this brief discussion it is better to center on the main issue. Our society is throwing out many an inherited set of rules and inhibitions. Some of these should have been thrown out long ago. The question is whether we will rediscover the meaning of sex or distort it to our great loss.

Sex, which often is commercial, mechanical, or trivial, can be personal. Sexual activity, which frequently is the outlet for pride or fear or hostility, can be the expression of faithful love.

That is the meaning of the traditional vows in which man and woman take each other, "for richer or for poorer, for better or for worse, in sickness and in health, to love and to cherish, until death us do part."

12 | A New Era in Self-Understanding

EACH PERSON is constantly telling the world around him who he is. He is also deceiving the world about himself. Usually he is quite ready to tell his name and a few facts. His appearance shows roughly his age and maybe something about his occupation, his tastes, and his standard of living. The clothes he wears, his posture, the photographer's smile he sometimes spreads over his face—these half reveal and half hide him.

We all stand to gain something and to lose something, or so we think, by communicating ourselves to others. Hence we try to be genuine, make an effort to be natural—or plan to make a good impression, work to appear friendly. Some aspects of ourselves we cannot hide; others we can and do hide.

More curiously we play the same game with ourselves. Half eager, half afraid to know ourselves, we both open up our hearts to the scrutiny of our minds and deceive ourselves. The man who understands himself is a rare creature.

Go back in history as far as possible and you find persons trying to understand themselves. All kinds of people have worked at the job. They include poets, prophets, philosophers, scientists, and artists.

Our modern world has immensely complicated the task of self-understanding. In some ways it has revolutionized the effort. In the nineteenth and twentieth centuries new sciences have arisen. They give us information that can help us in knowing ourselves. Sometimes these same sciences confuse us and make the job harder.

THINGS AND SOULS

The human race entered this modern world with many ideas of the self inherited from the past. As in the preceding chapter, I shall mention two such ideas—not because there are only two, but because two give us the polar points between which we can take our bearings.

The first idea is that man is a *thing*. He is an object that moves about in space. He is a body.

According to this theory people have been compared to marbles or to billiard balls on a table—except that they vary in size and toughness. As they move, they bang into each other. The biggest and toughest have the best of it.

Obviously this theory has hold of a bit of the truth. Whether it has the whole truth and nothing but the truth is another question. But it includes *a* truth that no one can afford to forget. In some respects a person is a thing in space. Sometimes, by recognizing that he is a thing, he understands himself better. Two objects—say, two cars—cannot occupy the same space; they make trouble when they try. Similarly two people cannot occupy the same space. They often try, for example on the bus at rush hour, but the effort is painful and it has its limits.

A man may not like it that he is a thing. He may prefer to think of himself as more ethereal, more exciting, more creative than a thing. But he cannot get away from the facts. If somebody bumps into him or steps on his toe, he knows that he is a thing.

But it is another matter to ask how far it helps in self-under-standing to say, "I am a thing. I am like a billiard ball." The fact is that, however much a person resembles a billiard ball, he differs from it far more. To say, "I am like a billiard ball," may involve a little self-understanding and a great misunderstanding.

Many thoughtful critics maintain that the modern world is making all of us more like things. They worry that we shove each other around and get shoved around, that we have to fit the system, that we lose freedom, that we treat other people like things and in the process turn ourselves into things.

Contemporary art has gone to work on this theme. In a drawing called "Parallel," for example, Henry Toledano shows two vaselike objects that look quite similar. A closer inspection reveals one to be human—barely human. The artist made this comment on his own drawing: "The man and the vase, the ani-mate and the inanimate, resemble each other very much. The joke is on man here. Man considers himself the crown of creation, but he is really empty, like a vase." [1]

Alongside this idea of man as a thing, the modern world has inherited a second conception of the self. This goes back at least to Plato in the fourth century B.C. It is the opposite of the first idea in every way. It sees man as a spiritual being, as a *soul*. This soul has no resemblance to an object in space.

As Socrates describes this idea, in one of Plato's writings, the soul is temporarily and regrettably lodged in a body. The real self is spiritual; somehow it gets located in a material body for a while.

The wise man is concerned only for the soul. He is not interested in eating and drinking, or in the pleasures of love. He tries to separate the soul, so far as he can, from its partnership in the body. This body is a nuisance. It is full of lusts and fears that infect the soul. A person can learn to some extent to live the pure life of the soul in this world. But complete purification comes only when the soul is separated from the body at death.[2]

---

[1] *Time*, May 10, 1954.

[2] Plato, *Phaedo*, 66-67. These are the same passages that I referred to in Chap. 11 for a description of a negative attitude toward sex.

The most persuasive argument for this belief is Socrates himself. Frequently he showed an attractive earthiness that does not accord with the theory. But because he believed he was a moral being rather than a thing, because he believed in freedom and responsibility, he would not compromise his convictions or yield to public pressure. He insisted upon asking questions and testing ideas until he died a hero's death. Billiard balls do not do that.

However there are great difficulties with this theory of the person. Surely our bodies are a source of joy as well as of pain. Something is wrong with a self-understanding that despises or ignores the body. Our bodies are so integral to our selves that we fool ourselves if we pretend that they are not important.

But the Platonic theory had great influence in later centuries. It entered the Christian church, although the Bible has a very different conception of the self. The prophets of the Old Testament and Jesus of Nazareth did not blame man's evil ways on his body. They emphasized that human beings, in their wonderful and their dreadful qualities, are both physical and spiritual. But the Platonic belief became so powerful in the church that to this day many people think it is the Christian belief.

THE ANIMAL-MAN

We have looked at two ideas of the self inherited by modern man: the self as a thing and the self as a soul. Let us turn to some of the new conceptions that the modern world has developed.

The first of these is connected with the scientific hypothesis of organic evolution. Charles Darwin was the great scientist who produced persuasive evidence that man is related to higher apes. This theory came as a great jolt to modern man. Perhaps it should not have shocked people so much. Perhaps the Bible should have made them familiar with the idea that man is made of the dust of the earth and is akin to the animals as well as to God.

But to many people the idea of evolution was irreverent and insulting. Some jumped from the hypothesis that man is descended from animals to the claim that man is nothing but an animal. Gilbert and Sullivan spoofed this idea in a song:

> Darwinian Man, though well behaved,
> At best is only a monkey shaved!

In the comic opera a woman sings this song, to show her disdain for men. But if men are animals, women are too. We are all in this together.

The idea that man is an animal, like every other idea of man, demands investigation. Just as we learn something when we understand that we are things, we also learn something when we realize that we are animals. Experimental psychology, going to work on animals, discovers some traits of human behavior.

One notable instance is the experimental work conducted by the great Russian scientist, Ivan Pavlov, with dogs. Pavlov started with the simple fact that meat makes a hungry dog's mouth water. That is a reflex action. The dog does not have to think about what is happening; his brain does not tell his mouth to water. When he smells meat, the saliva starts flowing.

Then Pavlov began to ring a bell every time he fed the dogs. The animals smelled the meat and heard the bell—and their glands turned out the saliva. After the dogs got used to this experience, Pavlov took the next step. He rang the bell without giving the dogs any meat. And the dogs' mouths watered. Normally the sound of a bell does not affect the salivary glands of a dog. But these dogs had developed *conditioned* reflexes.

People have conditioned reflexes too. Learning to drive a car requires the development of conditioned reflexes. Pavlov was too intelligent to argue that a human being is a dog, but he had shown that the behavior of dogs sometimes helps us to understand ourselves.

Today psychology students all over the country run experiments with rats. It is handier to use rats than dogs. Rats are smaller, they don't eat so much, they don't bark, and they breed faster. Also, people do not love rats the way they love dogs, so they are more willing to play tricks on them for the sake of science. Therefore, in order to learn about human nature, they study rats.

But the validity of this whole process depends on the assumption that men are like rats. So we must ask the question: How much and in what ways are men like rats? Part of the answer, no doubt, is that some men are more like rats than others. But then the answer gets more complicated. All of us have some similarity to rats—in the functioning of digestion, blood circulation, the nervous system and its conditioned reflexes. And all of us differ from rats. Setting aside all the easy quips, it is always possible to tell the difference between a man and a rat.

The common rat-psychology of our times can actually help us to self-understanding at those points where human behavior resembles the rat's. But it deceives us—unless we are careful to recognize the difference between men and rats.

THE MACHINE-MAN

Another idea of human nature has become more persuasive in recent years: Man is a machine. People have toyed with this idea in the past. Certainly there are mechanisms within the person—for example, the reflexes and conditioned reflexes we have just been thinking about. So every now and then somebody has argued that the person himself is a machine. Few people took the argument seriously until the twentieth century. Then the amazing new electronic computers led many to ask: Just what is the difference between a person and a machine?

The computers can solve problems that most of us cannot begin to answer and can solve them far faster than the most skillful men. They have "memories" less tricky than ours. They can predict weather, play checkers, control the processes on an assembly line. In many ways they have been getting more human all the time: they are even learning to make mistakes and to have "nervous breakdowns."

Education is one of the many fields where the machines are active. Machines can do much of the work that human teachers once did. But people still teach the machines—or "program" them, to use the technical phrase. So we have people teaching the machines, which learn to teach other people. What will happen as we build machines to teach the machines? Since a machine can both "learn" and "teach," will people, as students and teachers, become unnecessary? Educators occasionally wonder about that.

There have even been suggestions that machines will learn to reproduce themselves. A lot of people will have something to wonder about if that happens.

Norbert Wiener invented the word "cybernetics," coming from the Greek word for "helmsman," to point to the similarities between the "thinking" of machines and of men.[3] He sometimes worried, especially in his latter years, about one possibility: men may build machines that will get out of control and threaten the well-being of people—unless men decide what is good and carefully make the machines so that they will contribute to that good.[4]

A few years ago a specialist was proudly demonstrating one of the great new computers to the press. He showed how it could accomplish many things better than human beings. To every skeptical question his reply showed confidence in the powers of the machine. I took some comfort from the fact that the reporters still questioned *him;* the machine was not giving its own interviews. Then a reporter asked, "Is the machine conscious?" The expert answered, "I don't know what consciousness is."

There is the issue. I may as well admit that I do not know *exactly* what consciousness is—just as I do not know exactly what cosmic rays are—but I think consciousness and cosmic rays are important. It is in that area of consciousness—of visions, of purposes, of decisions made to achieve chosen goals, of love and sympathy, of self-awareness and concern for others—that our human grandeur lies. Machines can help us in self-understanding by reminding us of the electronic processes that are part of our own thinking and deciding; but they can fool us if they lead us to neglect our most human qualities.

FREUDIAN MAN

One further idea of the self, developed in the modern world, has been the most epoch-making of all. This idea comes from the genius, Sigmund Freud, who explored the inner life of man and

[3] Norbert Wiener, *Cybernetics* (Paris: Herrmann et Cie, 1948).

[4] Norbert Wiener, address at New York University Institute of Philosophy, reported in *New York Times,* May 18, 1959.

developed the art of psychoanalysis. A host of investigators have
followed the leads opened up by Freud. Some of them agree with
him in almost every detail; others differ on matters of basic understanding. But altogether they have changed the self-understanding of us all. Sometimes it seems that most of the population have become amateur psychiatrists. Even schoolchildren are
likely to pick up the vocabulary of the ego, the superego, and the
id; the libido and Oedipus complexes; inferiority complexes,
repression, and inhibitions. Countless people talk about themselves and their neighbors in terms of adjustment, aggression,
and maturity; or inferiority complexes, repressions, and inhibitions.

Some people, of course, dislike everything that Freud represents. In 1956, one of America's great churches, the Cathedral
of St. John the Divine, in New York City, sponsored a collo-
quium celebrating the one hundredth anniversary of Freud's
birth. The program ended with a service of thanksgiving for his
life and work. Some angry letters came to the cathedral, object-
ing to this commemoration of an atheist. The Dean of the Cathedral, now Bishop James A. Pike of California, answered the com-
plaints: "You say Freud *was* an atheist; well, he is not one
now."

Although Freud lived and died an atheist and although like
everybody else he made some mistakes, there are good reasons for
the church to be grateful for him. First, the church should appreciate truth, whether it is discovered by churchmen or by anybody
else. Second, some of Freud's insights into human nature are
remarkably akin to those in the Bible.

One of those points of kinship, curiously, is in Freud's com-
ments about God. Freud believed that the idea of God is the
work of an unhealthy human imagination. In a combination of
wishful thinking and fearful thinking, we project onto the universe our imagination of God. Then we worship this illusion or
try to make a deal with it so as to escape from the realities of
life.[5]

This criticism of religion is unmistakably familiar to those
who have studied the prophets of the Old Testament. They too

[5] Sigmund Freud, *The Future of an Illusion* (London: Hogarth, 1928).

say that the people are using foolish imaginations, that men take refuge in false ideas of God that enable them to escape from reality. In many respects Freud is a descendant of those prophets.

Of course, there is a major difference. Sometimes Freud, with a dogmatic spirit that was opposed to his own scientific method, made a sweeping denial of God that he could not support with evidence. (On occasion, to give him deserved credit, he recognized his weakness on exactly this issue.) The prophets, on the other hand, denied false gods while affirming faith in a God who demanded that they face reality, cleansed of wishful hopes and weakening fears.

I am not arguing that the believer in God can cozily agree with everything in Freud. There are serious differences. But believers can be grateful that Freud forces them to ask—even when it hurts—in what ways they use religion as an escape.

Another point of kinship between Freud and the biblical tradition comes in the understanding of how people act and think. Freud used clinical methods to discover the importance of the unconscious. Many impulses, buried in the life of every person, are responsible for our behavior. Life involves conflict between the destructive, antisocial drives and the demands of living with other people in a civilization.[6] We love to think of ourselves as rational beings, but we are less rational than we suppose. Often our reason works in the services of unconscious impulses. We have a great ability to use our reason to deceive ourselves about our real purposes and motives.

All this is, at many points, a scientific vindication of what the Bible expressed imaginatively. In the vivid language of the Scripture man thinks not simply with his mind but with his heart. His emotions well up from his viscera. He experiences conflicts between his deep, destructive impulses and his more generous purposes. He has an infinite capacity to twist the facts to suit his own desires and to deceive himself. Thus many of the

[6] Sigmund Freud, *Civilization and Its Discontents* (Garden City, N.Y.: Doubleday Anchor Book, 1958). Freud may have underestimated the social qualities in human nature and may have exaggerated the oppressiveness of civilization. But certainly the history of recent decades has reinforced his insight into the conflicts within human life.

insights of the Bible, of St. Augustine, and of Martin Luther receive their first scientific verification in modern psychology.

Again, I should point out, this concurrence of themes does not mean that everything has become harmonious between Freudians and men of biblical faith. I say only that the work of Freud and his followers has brought new possibilities for self-understanding and that these frequently have a peculiar aptness for those of us in the Jewish-Christian traditions.

But self-understanding is never easy. By this time we have learned that we can misuse psychology, just as we can misuse automation, prayer, or any other human activity. With the techniques of psychology we can manipulate other people destructively—as did Nazi Joseph Goebbels with his Ph.D. in psychology, or as do demagogues and some advertisers in America.

Or we can use a few ideas, stolen from psychology, to evade ourselves rather than to understand ourselves. People can talk glibly about guilt complexes in order to escape the reality of guilt, which is so terribly real in our society and in personal lives. They can blame their troubles on the mistakes their parents made in rearing them—instead of facing the mistakes they are making in rearing their children. They can make psychology itself into an illusory answer to all their problems, instead of taking responsibility for themselves and their behavior. The fault is not in psychology but in the human person who can make of psychology either an avenue to truth or an escape.

UNDERSTANDING AND BEING

Self-understanding is not easy in any world. Everywhere people are eager to fool us about ourselves, and we are usually eager to be fooled.

In ancient times the Socratic tradition bade man: "Know thyself." And the biblical tradition asked the question of God: "What is man that thou art mindful of him?" Throughout following centuries the wisest and best of men have sought self-understanding. The venture is not new. But the twentieth century has made it new in some respects. The momentum of history, which is reconstructing our society in so many ways, is reshaping the issues of self-understanding.

We have an advantage over the past in the knowledge and ideas that have come from modern thinking, especially from biology and psychology. We need every help that we can get, and we shall be wise to treasure these gains that the human race has taken so long to achieve. Since these gains bring with them built-in hazards, we shall also be wise to use them carefully.

With all that we can learn from modern discoveries, not everything is a matter of information. Persons come to self-understanding only as they meet other people, accept responsibility, work and love, worship and pray, enjoy life, and enter into commitments. One way to learn about personality is to live as a real person. One way to understand humanity is to be human.

13 | Living in the Anxiety of Change

THROUGHOUT THIS BOOK we have been looking into some of the processes of a swiftly changing world. We have examined several areas where history demands that society and individuals achieve new understanding and make new decisions. We have seen that the many issues of contemporary life are interrelated in the movement of mankind into a new kind of civilization. Now we can return to some basic issues of living in a time like our own—a time of opportunity and of threat, a time whose pains may be either death-pangs or birth-pangs.

UNEASE

During the curious presidential campaign of 1964 there was much talk about the strange uneasiness in American life. James Reston mentioned it in several of his columns. The *Wall Street Journal* noticed that both candidates were worried by it. Senator Barry Goldwater spoke about "a virtual despair among the many who look beyond material success to the inner meaning of their lives." President Lyndon B. Johnson recorded the feeling that "we haven't been keeping faith with tomorrow or with ourselves."

Walter Lippmann, a philosopher and the most eminent of American newspaper columnists, located the cause of the problem in the vast transformations of life that the modern world has brought:

> The malady is caused, I believe, by the impact of science upon religious certainty and of technological progress upon the settled order of family, class, and community. The "virtual despair" comes from being uprooted, homeless, naked, alone and unled. It comes from being lost in a universe where the meaning of life and of the social order are no longer given from on high and transmitted from ancestors but have to be invented and discovered and experimented with, each lonely individual for himself.[1]

In this situation Lippmann saw a lesson for both conservatives and liberals. Conservatives cannot try to preserve or return to old ways. Instead they have to "create the new forms in which the enduring truths and values can be carried on in a world that is being radically transformed." Liberals have to mature beyond the "primitive" liberalism that thought freedom would come with the overthrow of tyranny. They must undertake "the vast creative effort to invent and to make work the kind of authority and discipline and government under which free men can enjoy freedom."

Those persuasive words describe a momentous task for mankind. Although men are not ready for it, history will not let them wait. The human race often must undertake enterprises it is not ready for. That is part of the hazard and fascination of living.

In the first chapter of this book I said that important decisions come at the meeting place between faith and facts. Faith apart from facts does not tell men what to do or what courses of action to consider. Facts apart from faith can never convince men that love is better than fear or that courage is better than despair. Faith in the midst of facts—appreciating, ordering, and responding to facts—gives birth to insight and decision.

In the ancient world the dramatist Aristophanes, looking

---

[1] Walter Lippmann, in *New York Herald Tribune*, Aug. 4, 1964.

out upon a society where familiar traditions and patterns of life were disintegrating, wrote: "Whirl is king." That ancient world floundered, fought, and failed. New forces entered the world and reconstituted it. The Christian church gave the world a sense of order, an institutional stability, and a dominating presence that symbolized security.

That, I predict, will not happen again. The church should not be sad that it will not reclaim its medieval role. Then it served a temporary function, useful in its time, but quite different from the vocation of the church in the New Testament or in our time.

Faith now has a different calling. It must respond to history without becoming the mere echo of history. Any historical situation presents to faith both temptation and opportunity. So it is today.

FAITH AND COMFORT

Often religious faith has driven men to defy tyrants, to cross hazardous oceans and continents, to die for God and friends. Today people usually expect something different of faith. When religion achieves an established status, it comes to stand for the familiar and the comfortable. People look to it more for reassurance than for innovation.

In the contemporary world some people are making fortunes, others are getting hurt, and most people see little permanence. The prosperous white minority of mankind feels threatened by revolutions all over the world. Familiar ways of life are passing. Civilization could crumble in man-made earthquake, wind, and fire.

Naturally people crave security. Since their faith is inherited, they associate it with inherited ways. They are less interested that the church transform the world than that it be a reminder of stability. Often they ask their churches to provide havens from strife, to avoid the controversy that is inherent in biblical faith, to assure them that everything is all right even if this means crying "peace, peace" when there is no peace.

The temptation to apostasy is great. The church can distort its faith, offer protection rather than exposure to the world, pleasant fellowship rather than enlistment in a daring cause. The bond of unity in local churches may become more the congeniality of people from the same social class than commitment to a shared faith and mission. The deity whom men worship may be the symbol of comfort and safety rather than the God who calls for repentance and sacrificial service.

Then the church may retreat. One way of retreat is to resist the movement of history and try to live in the past—in a more rural America, in a medieval Christendom, in a biblical world where life was simpler. Its members may cling to old art and architecture, old legalisms, old hymns, old religious institutions. Even while in their secular life they drive their modern cars, watch television and eat frozen foods, and use all the achievements of modern medicine and industry, they may nostalgically orient their faith to a bygone world.

Or, knowing the impossibility of turning the clock back, the church and its members may try a second style of retreat—the retreat into the inner life. This method of resisting change has a deceptive plausibility. Has not faith always called men's attention to the inner human problems that no changing politics or economics can solve? The pious churchman can easily sort out the biblical texts that bid him be unspotted by the world and ignore the texts that call him to love the world as God loves it. His church can enjoy whatever affluence a modern economy brings it, while basically despising economic processes, ignoring political responsibilities, and ministering to men's souls. It may seek to help its members in their homes while ignoring them in their labor, their professions, their business careers. At best such a ministry is disastrously incomplete. At its worst it is a blasphemous corruption of the church's calling. The entertainment business has long known how to provide relaxation for tired businessmen. The church accepts a sardonic fate if it aspires to do the same for the more tame and genteel among modern men.

The impulse to seek comfort and stability in faith is not entirely wrong. Faith rightly seeks to live with an awareness of eternity. It rightly awakens compassion for the widow and the fatherless, for infants and the aged, for all who are weak and sinful—as all are weak and sinful. There is no one so strong that he can despise all comfort, if it is remembered that comfort means to strengthen as well as to protect.

But any profound faith asks of man's strength as truly as it gives to his weakness. It addresses him in his time and place, both awakening his memory of the past and directing him toward the future. In time of change faith belongs in the change, not waiting it out and not simply riding the wave of the future, but participating, guiding, struggling. The faith that is comfort is also courage. Or more accurately, it is comfort because it is courage.

FAITH AND COURAGE

The courage associated with faith is often the courage to resist temptation and to stand firm against opposition. Such courage is as important today as ever. But perhaps more important, and especially important today, is the courage to move, to innovate, to make decisions.

In the emerging society of our time the decisions that test faith are becoming more subtle and complex. It is not enough for the advertiser to avoid blatant lies; he must meet the issue of manipulating people to their harm. It is not enough for the industrialist to live up to his contracts; he must face up to the question of the responsible use of power. It is not enough for the United States to refrain from conquering colonial peoples; this nation must ask how its economic power helps or harms people whom most of us scarcely know about.

Ethical decisions increasingly call for inventiveness as well as firmness. Our society continuously develops new situations in which no codes and precedents, no high purposes and motives are enough. Only by combining sensitivity to human needs with rigorous understanding of intricate social processes can we make sound decisions instead of blundering or drifting.

H. Richard Niebuhr has compared ethical responsibility with the task of "the motor-car driver who must make forty decisions each minute. Neither obedience to rules of the road, nor desire to arrive at his goal, offers sufficient basis for his conduct." [2] The driver is not going to do better by forgetting his

[2] H. Richard Niebuhr, *The Responsible Self* (New York: Harper & Row, 1963), pp. 108-109.

goal or by neglecting the traffic rules, but these are not enough. He must meet situations as they arise, must improvise, must exercise his judgment. The task of our society and the people in it is even more challenging, because many of our travels are on uncharted roads where no patterns of traffic have been established.

Therefore ethical decisions of the future must increasingly be worked out by men and women at their jobs in a world of specialized but interrelated functions. The time is long past when medieval priests or puritan pastors could instruct their people in all the needful rules of behavior. There are, of course, still simple decisions of honesty or dishonesty, of fraud or fair play. But on these we scarcely need instruction, although we may need the will to act. The major ethical decisions of our time concern far-ranging issues of the use of power, the organization of production and distribution, the relation of men to machines, the establishing of freedom in an increasingly organized world, the maintenance of peace. These decisions must be made by the men who exercise power and live day in and day out in the midst of their responsibilities.

Such men need criticism and help from those who see issues from varied perspectives. They need the advice of the scientists who study society and human behavior. They need the support of communities of faith that nourish the religious imagination and sensitize the conscience. They need the prosaic wisdom of the citizenry as well as the insight of specialists. All mankind shares the risks of the new epoch of history, and all mankind has a right to participate in the shaping of that history.

Men of Christian faith may meet this new era with a peculiar zest. For as Christ lived in the flesh and ministered to flesh, it is their opportunity, living in flesh, to minister to the flesh of society—a society where flesh and blood are nourished by electronics and nuclear energy, by planes in the atmosphere and satellites in orbit, by printing presses and television beams. The modern society has its monuments, exalting and depressing: its education available to many and its vulgar mass communications, its wealth that both relieves suffering and pressures people to consume useless products, its racial understanding and its warfare, its breath-taking architecture and its urban rot, its invention of new skills and its destruction of old. In this world and no other God calls his people to obedience.

There was a time in Old Testament history when men wanted to build a temple for God. But God said No. He preferred to live in a tent, for he was a God on the move, a God not bound to a place. As time passed and society changed, God consented—so his people believe—to the building of a temple where he might dwell in the inmost holy of holies. This temple, some believed, was permanent; it would never be destroyed. They were mistaken. The buildings and social institutions built by men are never permanent. Life moves. Man is a historical being; the biblical God is a God of history. So the day came when men learned that God lives in a temple not made by hands.

That lesson mankind needed to learn. But the lesson was mislearned whenever people believed that God was uninterested in the work of their hands. God has created them as men of action, men driven by nature to economic and political achievements, men who in all that they do glorify or defy God.

So the times came when men once again made buildings for God—temples, cathedrals, churches. Sometimes they forgot that factories, theaters, schools, and capitols belong no less to God's world. They were happy to confine God within churches. And those churches, made sturdily of stone and brick, often became symbols of the permanence of God and of the society that built them. Now again God is showing humanity that he will not be held within the buildings or the social structures of the past.

If God dwells in a temple not made by hands, perhaps the God of the tents is nevertheless a more profound symbol for our age than the God of the temple. If today men build to his glory, they will use the steel and stone, the glass and plastics of modern society, not the animal skins of ancient tents. But they will know that their building and all their human institutions are fragile and temporary. The God of history is on the move. A people who serve him will be a people on the move.

Acknowledgments

BECAUSE THIS BOOK originated in a series of television programs, many people contributed to its development. I should start by thanking Dr. Everett C. Parker, Director of the Office of Communication of the United Church of Christ, who was instigator and producer of the series. His associates, William Winslow and Dr. S. Franklin Mack, contributed many ideas to the production. The director of the shows, Richard R. Rector, and his assistant, Miss Maury Clark, were constantly helpful. All these people through their imagination and their criticism helped to shape my thinking, yet allowed me freedom to resist them and follow my own leads.

A number of interviews were an integral part of the original series. They are not preserved in the book, but ideas that came out of the interviews are now part of the book. I am grateful to the many specialists who showed a wonderful good faith in letting me tap their professional wisdom, then make my own use of it. They are not responsible for what I have written, but they have enriched it with their knowledge. The following list indicates the people I interviewed and the chapters to which their thinking is related:

Chapter 2. Richard O. Grisdale, a scientist on the technical staff of Bell Telephone Laboratories, Murray Hill, N.J. Dr. Harold K. Schilling, Professor of Physics and Dean of the Graduate School, Pennsylvania State University.

Chapter 5. Ashby Bladen, former Executive Vice-President, Aetna Insurance Company, and former President, New York Board of Trade.

Chapter 7. Dr. Charles Lawrence, Department of Sociology and Anthropology, Brooklyn College. Three of the ministers of the Riverside Church, New York City: Dr. Robert J. McCracken, Senior Minister; the Rev. Robert Polk, Minister to Youth; the Rev. Pablo Cotto, Hispano-American Minister.

Chapter 8. The Hon. Donald W. Webber, Associate Justice, Supreme Judicial Court of Maine.

Chapter 10. The Hon. Adlai E. Stevenson, United States Ambassador to the United Nations.

Chapter 11. Mary Steichen Calderone, M.D., former Medical Director, Planned Parenthood–World Population; now with the Sex Information and Education Council of the United States.

Chapter 12. Professor James Crane, Department of Art, Florida Presbyterian College.

The book includes adapted portions of an address delivered at the National Study Conference on the Church and Economic Life, called by the National Council of Churches, in Pittsburgh, Penn., in 1962; and of an address at the Conference on Religion and Urbanization of the Frank L. Weill Institute for Studies in Religion and the Humanities, in Cincinnati, Ohio, in 1963.

I have also incorporated fragments of other papers prepared for the Department of Church and Economic Life of the National Council of Churches, and the Department on Church and Society of the World Council of Churches. This book echoes themes that I have written about in *The Nation, Christianity and Crisis,* and *Social Action;* but I think I have not repeated these writings specifically.

To all the people, institutions, and journals that I have listed I am grateful for stimulating my thought.

Quotations from the Bible are from the Revised Standard Version, copyrighted by the Division of Christian Education of the National Council of Churches.

R. L. S.